AFFIRMATION LIFE TOOLS

70 ways to cope with chemo and other medical treatments

DR ANNE MARIE EVERS

Inside Out Media

ISBN 978-1-928103-06-6

Edited by Olga Sheean
www.olgasheean.com

Cover and design by Lewis Evans
www.lewisevans.net

Produced by InsideOut Media
www.insideoutmedia.net

Also by the author and available in hard copy and e-book form at www.amazon.com and www.amazon.ca:
- *Affirmations: Your Passport to Happiness, 8ᵗʰ Edition*
- *Affirmations: Your Passport to Lasting, Loving Relationships*
- *Affirmations: Your Passport to Prosperity/Money*
- *Affirmation Toolbox*
- *Affirmation Beauty Book*

Dr Anne Marie Evers is also a co-author of the #1 best-selling series, *Wake Up and Live the Life you Love in Spirit*, with Dr Wayne Dyer, Dr Deepak Chopra and others.

Queries regarding rights and permissions should be sent in writing to the following fax number or e-mail address:

Fax: 604-904-1127
E-mail annemarieevers@shaw.ca
Website: www.annemarieevers.com

Contents

Acknowledgements

I wish to acknowledge and thank the following people for their love and support when I was writing this special book: my son, David Evers, and his wife, Lorna; my daughter, Aren Evers, and her husband, Dario Dusman; and my sister, Darlene O'Neill.

I wish to remember my beloved late husband Reginald (Reggie) Clemens for his tremendous love, support and humour during the first part of my healing journey. Sadly, he passed away in the middle of my chemo treatments. I wish to thank his family for their continued caring and support.

Special thanks to: Deborra Harney-Gregor for performing the Life Celebration for Reginald and for the most helpful grief counselling she provided, and is continuing to provide for me weekly; Marci Harriott for the many weekly uplifting and healing Reiki treatments she gave me in my home; Heike Bogner for faithfully coming to my home and doing my hair every week; and the wonderful friends who were with me during my challenging journey: Rose Marcus, Sadna Lal, Rob King, Peter and Kate Williams, and a great number of other wonderful people.

Thank you to Christine Einarson for her hours of help. Thanks also to Ruth Ellen Peters for her help and support. I wish to thank the doctors and nurses at Lions Gate Hospital, North Vancouver, BC—particularly my wonderful doctor, Sasha Smiljanic, and his staff, Pat MacDonald, and the many wonderful volunteers and personnel in the chemo department.

Thanks also to my editor, Olga Sheean, and designer, Lewis Evans, for their excellent work.

Special appreciation to:

Iris Enkurs, Social Worker at Lions Gate Hospital, North Vancouver, BC, who believed in me and my teachings and supported me in setting up monthly lectures at the hospital on affirmation tools to help other patients cope with the effects of chemo and/or other medical treatments. Thank you also, Iris, for paving the way for me to lecture and create an Affirmation Life Tool Program for Hospice. I am extremely grateful to you for helping me through the most difficult health and grief challenges of my life, and for acknowledging and observing the positive results obtained by chemo patients when they regularly use these Affirmation Life Tools. When I, too, witnessed the positive effects of these tools, it gave me a renewed passion and zest for teaching these important concepts. You were the catalyst that made it all happen!

Lastly, I would like to thank all those who use the principles and concepts taught in my books and the thousands of men and women who, over the past 25 years, have allowed me to guide them in their search for a happier and healthier life. I greatly appreciate your valuable feedback, e-mails, letters and telephone calls of encouragement. Thank you for sharing your many affirmation success stories with me. I am very blessed to have you all in my life!

Affirmations when properly done always work!
(although not always within our preferred time frame or the way we think they should work)

Dedication

I dedicate this book to those who are
undergoing chemo and/or other
challenging medical treatments,
as well as to their families and friends,
and to the wonderful doctors and nurses
who help us through these
medical challenges and traumatic times.

With warm affirmation blessings,

Dr Anne Marie Evers
Spring 2015

Disclaimer

The information provided in this book is for educational purposes only and is not intended to be used, nor should it be used, to diagnose or treat any medical condition. For diagnosis or treatment of any medical problem, consult your physician.

Neither the publisher nor the author is responsible for any health issues that may require medical supervision, or liable for any damages or negative consequences from any treatment, action, application or preparation of these Affirmation Life Tools to any person following the suggested practices in this book.

You are advised to talk to your doctor and/or healthcare professional about your specific medical condition and/or treatments. The information in this book may be helpful, but it is not a substitute for medical advice. Everyone experiences chemotherapy and/or radiation treatments differently, depending on their age, sex, general health, lifestyle, the medication used and many other factors.

Foreword

By Bernie Siegel, MD

I'd like to share with you my personal experience with affirmations. My wife and I start the day doing some exercises to help her cope with multiple sclerosis. While we climb a flight of stairs, I repeat the following affirmations: "Thank you for everything. I have no complaint whatsoever. I am happy. I am healthy. I love my life, family, body and pets. I am content with what I have. I rejoice in the way things are. I have all the energy and strength that I require. Nothing is lacking. The whole world belongs to me."

When we face emotional or physical problems, words can become swords that can kill or cure because what the mind believes the body experiences. I know from personal experience how our attitude and life events contribute to our health and vulnerability to illness. Yet oncologists often do not see or believe this because they treat a diagnosis and not their patients' experience. As Jung said, "The diagnosis may help the doctor but it doesn't help the patient. [...] the key thing is the story, for it alone shows human background and human suffering and only at that point can the doctors' therapy begin to operate."

Decades ago, psychologist Bruno Klopfer correctly predicted the rate of growth of cancers in 20 out of 24 patients, based on their personality profiles. Psychiatrists, too, understand the benefits of transformation and many have seen supposedly terminal cancer patients recover when they received therapy to prepare them for the end of their life. Even hospices have dropouts and graduations.

Mind and body are a unit and I have learned that we can generate health by having beliefs and affirmations with a positive outlook. It's really about having hope and conviction in your body's innate capacity to heal itself.

False hope is an oxymoron; hope is always real. So believe, have faith and let the affirmations in this book turn words into swords that can help cure you and eliminate your illness and problems. Become a health warrior, with Anne Marie as your guide and life coach through the troubled waters of cancer and chemo. You can dance in the rain.

I know that affirmations, when properly done, make a life-changing difference. Read on, learn and live.

Introduction

Book summary

This book is designed to help you through your entire healing journey and beyond. It will be your companion, from the moment you receive a diagnosis, until you resume a healthy, normal life—assisting, guiding and supporting you during your treatments and their side effects, and throughout your recovery.

To facilitate your journey, the book contains the following elements:
- a directory of negative side effects and Affirmation Life Tools for coping with the effects of chemo and other challenging medical treatments (in alphabetical order);
- guidelines for using the coping and healing power of Affirmation Life Tools;
- an explanation of the affirmation process—what affirmations are and how they work;
- my own personal journey of healing from colon cancer, severe infection, chemo and the death of my beloved husband;
- ways of coping with the fear that often accompanies the negative side effects of chemo;
- a section relating to caregiving, family, career and money issues resulting from medical challenges;
- the Affirmation Life Tools that I used and am still using, with great success.

Using the word 'negative'

Although the side effects of drugs are generally considered to be 'negative', they can sometimes have unintended benefits—such as causing the loss of excess weight that one might have been struggling with for years, or creating a strong dislike for certain foods and beverages that subsequently turn out to be allergens that have been causing some serious health issues.

In the medical profession, a 'negative' report is a *good* thing, indicating that a particular condition or disease is not present in the person being tested. A positive report indicates that the disease or medical condition is present in the body. In this book, I focus on the *positive* effects of positive statements, exercises, practices, affirmations and more, to encourage you along the way!

Start right now

The Affirmation Life Tools in this book are created and tailored specially for health issues and for dealing with depression, fear, pain and distress. But they can also be used for other areas of your life—and you can start right here and right now! No searching for hours on the Internet or waiting for a package to be delivered. Use them for whatever you wish to manifest. Always be certain to add the safety clause, 'to the good of all parties concerned', and that includes you! If you're dealing with a change in career, a lay-off, a relationship break-up, a move, a difficult boss/employer, family problems, the search for a partner, or financial difficulties, use these Affirmation Life Tools. See where they might be applicable to different parts of your life and go for it!

Entertain a new point of view

Has someone ever suggested that you try something new and a little unconventional, but you'd never thought about it or felt it would work for you? I know I have. But if you're willing to embrace and use these Affirmation Life Tools, coupled with your commitment to bring about the vibrant health, joy, success and happiness that you so desire and deserve, you can make it happen.

We all want to be heard

One young lady who was diagnosed with cancer and underwent chemotherapy asked me to publish her personal appeal to those who know other individuals with cancer.

Please do not look at us with pity in your eyes and say something like, "Oh, you poor thing. I suppose you will have to quit your job. Can you still keep your house? How will you manage?" We are people just like you and we do not want to be pitied. We are strong, courageous people who are in the fight of our lives to survive! Yes, we want your love, caring and sympathy but not your pity. Thank you, Anne Marie, for allowing me to share this important message with your readers.

Getting the most out of this book

Read the whole book once and get acquainted with it. Then re-read it, allowing the words and the principles that resonate with you to become your trusted and loyal friends. Allow them to sink deep into your subconscious mind so they can take root, grow and manifest your desires, as affirmed. I say my very own affirmation at the end of every chapter in my books: Affirmations when properly done always work! I add a note about timing, however, as whatever we wish for might not be what's best for us, at that moment, or we may not be ready to deal with it in a healthy way. Doing affirmations therefore requires that we trust that things will unfold when the time is right.

Although these Affirmation Life Tools have created wondrous miracles and desired results for many, I want to stress that sometimes they may not work within your time frame or as you think they should. If that happens, do not give up! Keep on using them, as the answer or desired result could be just around the corner.

There are different Affirmation Life Tools for different side effects, for things that you would like to control, and for things that you desire to have in your life. Jot down any information or affirmations that relate to what's going on for you, and use the Affirmation Life Tools with as much excitement, faith and expectancy as you can (even if you don't yet trust that they will work).

Affirmations when properly done always work!
(although not always within our preferred time frame or the way we
think they should work)

PART ONE

The affirmation process

Welcome to the wonderful world of powerful
Affirmation Life Tools, where dreams really can and do
come true! This is the home of positive thinking, healing, miracles,
creative visualization, mind power, forgiveness, random acts of
kindness and much more!

My name is Anne Marie Evers. I am a colon cancer/chemo survivor, ordained minister and Doctor of Divinity—*not* a medical doctor. All the information in this book is taken from my own life experiences and from testimonials and e-mails from the thousands of readers worldwide who have successfully used affirmations to make their lives happier, healthier and more prosperous. I do not prescribe; I only suggest and encourage you to try some of the Affirmation Life Tools shared here—especially the ones that have helped me immensely with the negative side effects from my recent colon cancer and chemotherapy journey.

My story

Many years ago, when my son David was born with crooked feet, and long before I knew about affirmations, it turned out that I was doing one of the most important affirmations of my life! I used to look at David sitting in his high chair and say to him, "David, you will walk!" I repeated this statement over and over many times during the day. I told family members and friends that David would walk. Some looked at me with pity and others laughed and said I should be more realistic. We were poor and the doctor said it would take many thousands of dollars to fix his feet, but my belief and positive statements never wavered. A vision of him walking normally was firmly rooted in my mind and I was not the least bit concerned about how that might happen. I just knew that it would.

At the time, we had a small coffee shop and one of our regular customers, Donald, came in one day and said, "What is wrong with the little fella?" David was sitting in his high chair in the coffee shop and anyone could see how deformed his feet were. Three days later, Donald appeared again and announced that he was a Shriner and he had arranged to have David brought down to the Shriners Hospital for Children in Spokane, Washington for the necessary surgery to make his feet normal so that he could walk. I was overjoyed and so thankful for this wonderful organization. So I mustered the courage to take my eight-month-old son in a car with a stranger (one of the Shriners) to the Children's Hospital in Spokane and leave him there in the hospital's care. He was there almost a year. When he came home, I had to regularly perform certain exercises on his feet, and every year for 15 years or so, we had to make the trip to Spokane for follow-up or further treatment.

I am so glad that I, as a mother, accessed that burning desire and faith that it would happen. I also breathed life into my affirmation by taking action: talking to Donald about my son's condition. Miracles do happen when we firmly believe, affirm, take the appropriate action and accept the answer.

The five building blocks of the affirmation process

The affirmation process that I teach is built on the following five building blocks:

1. Forgiveness

True forgiveness heals even the deepest of wounds. When you truly forgive self and/or others, you never have to do it again. Forgiveness is very powerful. When you forgive, your energy changes the physical structure of your cells and DNA. To have and maintain radiant health, true forgiveness is essential.

2. Conscious, positive thoughts

What is the greatest power that has ever been discovered? Nuclear energy? The power of wealth or fame? I believe it is the power of your thoughts, words and mind. When thoughts are held in the mind, they take on a life of their own and attract other similar thoughts. This is why it is so important to think positive thoughts of healing, health, joy and happiness instead of negative thoughts of worry, sickness, disease or unhappiness. There are two ways of creating our reality: consciously programming what we want out of life or simply accepting what comes our way. When we consciously think thoughts of healing, health and well-being, we are consciously programming our life.

3. Mind power

You have one mind with two distinct, yet interrelated, functional characteristics:

- the conscious, objective, outward or waking state;
- the subconscious, subjective, inward or sleeping state.

I liken the conscious mind to the captain of a ship who gives the orders, and the subconscious mind as the crew who obey the captain's orders immediately and without question. How are you instructing your subconscious mind? Perhaps it is time to check whether the captain of your ship is giving orders of continued abundant health, well-being, joy and happiness.

The following two stories demonstrate the amazing power of the subconscious mind.

BRUCE'S TRANSFORMATION FROM DISEASE TO HEALTH

Bruce was diagnosed with lung cancer and given 6 months to live. When his doctor told him the news, Bruce was shocked but then accepted it. He resigned from his job, made out his will, put his finances in order, and retreated from life. He did not leave his house and refused to eat properly. He lost weight and became weak and sick. He was just waiting to die.

A few months later, Bruce received a call from the doctor's nurse, saying that it was imperative that he come in immediately to speak with the doctor. When Bruce shuffled into the doctor's office, he looked and acted like a sick, dying, old man. His doctor said, "Bruce, I don't know how to tell you this but there's been a terrible mistake. The X-rays got mixed up and the one I read was not yours. You are not dying of lung cancer. In fact, according to your X-rays, you're in good health! I'm very sorry and I cannot explain this mix-up."

Bruce was stunned and shocked! He asked for proof that he really was healthy. When he finally accepted the fact that he did not have lung cancer, his whole body and attitude changed. The nurse in the reception area could not believe her eyes. The sick, unhappy man who had hobbled into the doctor's inner office was certainly not the same man who came bouncing out half an hour later. Such was the power of Bruce's mind.

Even though he had been healthy all along, he had generated negative thoughts that actually made him sick and depressed. When he realized he was healthy, Bruce switched his mind into a mode of good health and transformed himself in accordance with those positive, happy, healthy thoughts. He began living life to the fullest, from that very moment, and has since married and started a family.

THE CAT

When I was a real estate agent, I had a client who was adamant that I only show her houses or townhouses that did not have animals—especially cats—as she was very allergic to them. During one showing, she suddenly dropped onto the couch and started sneezing and getting watery eyes. I was shocked and asked her if she was okay. She looked up at me and said, "I thought I told you not to show me any place that had cats!" I looked at her in amazement and said, "But, Audrey, there is no cat here!" She jumped up, ran to the master bedroom, pointed to the bed and said, "What's that?" I went and picked it up and brought it over to her. It was a stuffed cat. Such was the power of her subconscious mind that it gave her the actual physical symptoms of an allergy to cats when there was no cat present.

Never underestimate the power of your subconscious mind to produce a physical result.

4. Affirmations

Whenever you are goal-setting with powerful, focused intent, you are doing a form of affirmation. Use the power of properly done affirmations to bring healing, health, well-being and happiness into your life. Affirmations are your orders to the universe to help you co-create what you desire.

5. Creative visualization

Creative visualization is a structured, directed process of imagining images in your mind. The images your mind receives from your mental world are just as real as those from an event that's actually taking place. When you practise creative visualization, you are mentally transporting yourself into the future, into a situation that has not yet taken place. This is what I did when I was lying in the hospital bed with cancer. I visualized stepping ahead into the future where I was well, visiting with family and friends, writing my books, hosting my radio shows, lecturing and doing all the things that I love. I made the pictures in my mind vivid, colourful and very real—as if they were actually taking place. And that reality manifested exactly as I affirmed!

When you have all five building blocks firmly in place, you have a strong and solid foundation upon which to build your own powerful affirmations.

What are affirmations?

Affirmations are similar to prayers, wishes or goals, only they are more structured and specific. To affirm is to make firm and, simply put, the basis of all affirmations is positive thinking. When people tell me they have never done an affirmation, I ask them if they have ever blown out candles on a birthday cake and made a wish. If they say they have, then I tell them they have done an affirmation. It's as simple as that!

Affirmations are also commands or decrees, and using them is like submitting your orders to the universe. They can also be called self-talk—what we say to ourselves about ourselves—which has a huge impact on our subconscious mind and, consequently, on what we attract in life.

Affirmations are natural. Whenever you are setting a goal or planning for a particular outcome with powerful, focused intent, you are actually doing a form of affirmation. Whether or not you are conscious of doing affirmations, you have done many in your lifetime. You may call it goal-setting, planning, wishing or praying.

Author Kate Large (TheGameofLifeMastery.com) puts it this way:

Affirmations are statement-containers of profound, deep energy.
That is why you word your affirmation in such a way that it
HOLDS the energy you wish to BE in!

Affirmations ascend the power of your words to a new extraordinary
level! Affirmations worded properly are the muscle to shape your
creative energy and manifest what you want into your reality.

Master affirmations

A master affirmation is an affirmation that incorporates all of the elements of your wish or desire, and it may be several lines long. This is the first step in creating your own affirmation for a particular purpose. Once you have clearly defined your affirmation, with all the relevant details, you can use it as the basis for a short-form affirmation.

Short-form affirmations

Short-form affirmations consist of several key words from your master affirmation that you can jot down several times a day and/or regularly repeat out loud during the day to keep that request (affirmation) on the front burner of your mind.

What are Affirmation Life Tools?

During my recent health challenge, I created and developed very effective Affirmation Life Tools for restoring my health, combining my teachings of affirmations with powerful key words and specially designed exercises. I am still using these tools to get rid of some residual side effects. I have given them the following notice: "Your services are no longer required. You must leave now!" I am happy to report that they are slowly but surely leaving my body, as instructed. It is my hope that you will find many of these tools helpful on your own journey to wellness.

I have been successfully teaching the wondrous power of properly done affirmations worldwide for many years, through my books, e-books, writings, radio/Internet shows and lectures.

I will share my own experience with you in a very real and down-to-earth way—as if we were sharing a cup of tea or coffee and chatting. I will also remind you of the power of our self-talk and how important it is to avoid saying negative things to ourselves, about ourselves, and to others. We live in a world of universal laws, one of which is the law of attraction, which states:

> What you think about, you bring about. More gathers more.
> Like attracts like. What you are seeking is seeking you.

This law of attraction is always in operation; you cannot turn it off. It works for every single person the same way, regardless of their circumstances.

Affirmations work within the law of attraction, attracting to us what we are affirming, mentally or physically.

Research

I have done a fair amount of research on the side effects of chemotherapy and ways to alleviate them, but I have found very little information dealing specifically with positive mental self-talk or affirmations. Much has been written about the body–mind connection, and we are daily learning more about the power of the subconscious mind and its impact on our lives. We all have at our disposal a powerful mind that we can use to direct the course of our health, outlook and fulfillment. Although our minds may be deeply programmed with limiting beliefs that hinder our progress, we can choose to change our minds and think positive new thoughts. Choosing to embrace these Affirmation Life Tools to accelerate and improve your own health and well-being will also have a positive impact on others, inspiring them to trust in their own ability to heal and manifest what they desire. It is a conscious choice, and you must decide what feels right for you.

Cutting-edge Affirmation Life Tools

I truly believe that these simple, yet effective and proven Affirmation Life Tools will become one of the cutting-edge tools in healthcare. I am happy to be a pioneer in this process, and I continue to learn as I create, use and review the tools. Both the tools and I are a work in progress, constantly evolving.

Having experienced such profound breakthroughs in using these tools myself, I felt compelled to share them with as many people as possible.

How to create an effective master affirmation

Meditate before doing your master affirmations

Before creating and saying your master affirmations, it's important to sit quietly, clear your mind and relax. Take several deep breaths, breathing out fear, disbelief and negativity, and breathing in love, faith, vibrant health, healing and joy. Become very clear and specific about what you desire. When affirming for health issues, it's important to actually imagine and feel those healthy thoughts in your heart and trust that what you're affirming is being directed to the right places in your body.

When we make negative or positive statements, they go out into the universe and, through the ever-active Law of Attraction, they attract more of those same kinds of thoughts. So be very careful about what you're thinking and the words you speak, bearing in mind that every thought and word has an impact. Choose to say loving, positive words to yourself and, of course, treat all others with love and respect.

The importance of being specific

A master affirmation is your complete order to the universe. It should be specific, stating exactly what you desire. If you ordered a dress or shirt from the Sears catalogue and just said, "Please send me a dress or shirt," they would contact you asking you for more specific details—such as the catalogue number, quantity, colour, price etc, so they could successfully fill your order. The same is true of your master affirmation. Making it specific also makes it more real to you.

The following story, sent to me by one of my affirmation students, demonstrates the importance of being very specific with all of your affirmations:

I just have to share my story. When I did an affirmation for the perfect, lasting, successful career for me, it was not happening. I started to get discouraged. I shared my frustration at one of your affirmation meetings, and asked: "Why is my affirmation not working? I'm doing everything you teach and I really do want that perfect, lasting, successful, part-time career/position." You laughed and said: "Anna, you are not asking for what you desire. I just heard you say the words, 'part-time' and those words are not in your affirmation!" Well, I changed that and, several weeks later, I was working in that wonderful, lasting, successful, part-time position. I learned how important it was to add those words to my affirmation and how they were keeping me from realizing my desire. I urge others to be very specific and say exactly what they want! Thank you, Dr Evers, for turning on the light for me.

Being very clear about what you want is important. You know the 'what' and the universe knows the 'how'. It does not try to figure out what you want, but immediately goes to work preparing the conditions for your affirmation to manifest as affirmed.

You can modify, change, delete and/or add to your master affirmations as you change and become clearer about what you want in life. And you can always create a new one.

When you have created your master affirmation, dated and signed it, put it in a plastic insert sheet to keep it clean. Place each master affirmation in its own plastic insert sheet. It is important to fully do the affirmation process for each affirmation, focusing on one at a time.

To further focus and activate your subconscious mind, place a picture or sketch of your desired outcome or thing at the top of the page. This also helps to generate positive feelings. Every time you look at this image, you are reminded of what you're manifesting and how wonderful it looks.

The importance of engaging your five physical senses

When doing any affirmation or using any affirmation tool, engaging your five senses makes it extremely powerful. Take out your Master Affirmation and read it over every morning and evening. Then step ahead in your mind, several days, weeks, months or even years, and bring in your five physical senses, as outlined in the following process.

See what you are affirming as having already happened.
Hear people commenting on your wonderful success.
Feel how happy and excited you are.
Smell your favourite flower scent or perfume/cologne.
Taste some fresh, sparkling water or visualize taking a bite of a juicy apple.

Act as if what you are affirming has already happened! Enjoy your creation, in your imagination, as if it already exists.

Safety clause: to the good of all parties concerned (and that includes you!)

Sometimes, affirmations do not manifest within our preferred time frame or in the way we think they should. This is why I always add the safety clause (to the good of all parties concerned) so that, if what you are affirming is not for your highest good or for the highest good of all concerned, it will not manifest in that particular manner. It will find a different and better way to manifest.

If, for example, you are affirming for yourself abundant health, you could be led to see a particular doctor or healthcare practitioner, or find a medical treatment, product or modality that leads to the manifestation of that abundant health.

Change and revise your affirmations as often as necessary. As you change, your affirmations may need to change. Make adjustments and allow for the unexpected. Welcome new ideas and be self-disciplined and persistent. Perseverance means hanging in there when all the odds appear to be stacked against you.

Sample master affirmation
(Your order to the universe)

Make it specific, stating exactly what you desire.
Place your coloured picture or sketch of your desire here, at the top of the page

I, [*your name*], deserve and now have...
OR
I, [*your name*], deserve to be and now am...

_____

_____

_____

_____

to the good of all parties concerned.

I fully accept. Thank you, thank you, thank you.

Signed_____Dated_____

Note: When you create this master affirmation and date and sign it, you have made a firm and binding contract with God/the creator, the universal mind, your higher self or whomever/whatever you believe in.

Whenever the word *God* is used here, it refers to the universal mind, the creator, or whatever higher power you believe in. The process of doing affirmations is not a cult or any form of brainwashing. It is not 'black magic'. It is a completely real and natural process. You are simply working with the laws of the great universe. You make your own magic by using your own wondrous, inner creative power.

Affirmation rules

Affirmations are so powerful that care must be taken when using them, as per the following instructions:

- Never hurt or take from anyone and never wish anyone ill.
- Every master affirmation must contain the 'safety clause': to the good of all parties concerned.
- It must be personal, positive and in the present tense (the 3Ps); if you say, 'will have,' you are putting the manifestation off until some unspecified future time.
- Say 'Thank you' three times. When you give thanks in advance, you are anticipating success, which alerts the universe to your willingness to receive good things.
- Be specific, stating exactly what you desire.
- Always create a separate page for each of your master affirmations.
- Place each signed and dated master affirmation in a separate plastic insert sheet.
- Make your master affirmation colourful, as colour wakes up and excites the subconscious mind.
- Have fun!

Breathe life into your affirmations by taking action

You can stand in an elevator all day long and affirm that it goes to the desired floor, but until you or someone else pushes the button for that floor, nothing happens. When doing affirmations for your health, be sure to take the appropriate action.

Find out as much as possible about your condition and search the Internet and other places for information about products, modalities and/

or practitioners that might help you with that condition. Become proactive with your health and let the universe know that you mean business.

Timing

Affirmations can—and sometimes do—manifest immediately, as if by magic. At other times, they take longer, requiring our patience. Instant healing and miracles do occur, and we may wish for them to take place in our lives. I believe that this kind of healing depends a great deal on one's belief system and one's faith that it can happen. Don't get discouraged if you don't see immediate results; just imagine your manifestation being just around the corner. Keep on using your Affirmation Life Tools with faith, expectancy and excitement. One short-form affirmation that I did during my health challenge (and continue to do) is: "I am a patient person." Also, if I had not gone though this particular health challenge, I would not be writing this book today and sharing information that I have learned and used to help myself.

ABCs of health

It is a good idea to be proactive and to take responsibility for finding out all you can about the health challenge you are facing.

Accept responsibility for your health by learning and understanding as much as you possibly can about the nature of the condition with which you have been diagnosed. Always be conscious of what YOU can do to assist your body in cleansing, healing and revitalizing.

Be yourself and trust yourself. You are unique and this pain and/or cancer challenge may hold some hidden blessings or lessons that will ultimately enhance your life, if you are open to trusting the healing process.

Cleanse your mind and body of unhealthy emotions such as fear—the fear that this pain or health challenge is permanent or that you might not survive it. Know and say to yourself: "This is only a temporary condition," and then use the wonderful phrase that I use constantly: "This too shall pass"—and it does!

Affirmations can take time. By doing them regularly, you increase your faith, bringing healing and health consciousness into your being, personality, life and world. Almost everyone I meet is eager to find out when things are going to happen. When, when, when? To get an answer from your subconscious mind as to approximately when your affirmation could manifest, you can do the following visualization.

Close your eyes and visualize four circles, with time frames written beneath them, as follows:

- First circle—**Immediate**
- Second circle—**6 months**
- Third circle—**12 months**
- Fourth circle—**Other**

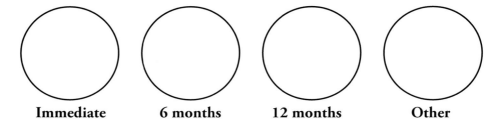

| Immediate | 6 months | 12 months | Other |

Mentally think of the affirmation that you wish to manifest now. Ask the question of how long it will take and *visualize* the answer going into one circle. Do not send it or force it. Just allow it to go in on its own. This process works best if you allow yourself to be the silent observer, *simply watching* it going into one of the circles. If it does not want to go into any circle, do the process again or wait for a while, as your subconscious mind may not be ready to answer.

If your mind takes you into the '12 months' or 'Other' circle, it may be that this is simply how it is at this moment. Do the exercise again in a few days or weeks. By then, things may have changed.

Learn from the lowly seed

The lowly seed puts its roots and tiny tendrils down into the rich, fertile soil of the earth. It takes root and grows. At the same time, it sends sprouts up towards the light. When it encounters any obstacles, as it undoubtedly does, it is not discouraged. Instead, it simply goes around them, always stretching towards the life force of the sun and the air.

The little seed shows no lack of faith, nor does it question the length of time it will take to manifest as a plant or tree. It simply acts, trusting in nature and the laws of the great universe. A seed of faith, once planted, never dies. The tiny seed is programmed. It puts all its energies into bringing its inherent blueprint into materialization. It knows, trusts and acts. It produces without question, fear or delay. Like seeds, affirmations have a timetable of their own.

The process of doing affirmations and using these Affirmation Life Tools is a growth process. The knowledge of how to produce and create loving relationships, health, healing, prosperity, wealth and happiness in your life was placed in you before you were born. This knowledge is activated through practising the appropriate affirmation tools.

Affirmations recorded in your own voice

I found it very helpful and soothing to listen to my own voice as a recorded affirmation. I created and voiced several recordings that I listen to every evening. I alternate between them so it doesn't get boring. I turn the recording on just as I am going to sleep and let it play until it ends a half hour or so later. It clicks off by itself. I have read, and I do believe, that our own voice is most in tune with our subconscious mind and helps our desires (affirmations) manifest quicker.

Allow the words of your recording to sink deep into your subconscious mind so they can take root, grow, and manifest your desire.

Some voice recording samples for you to use (or you can make up your own):

I love using my powerful Affirmation Life Tools daily.
My body is so relaxed and peaceful.
I have a deep, healthy and peaceful sleep and wake up feeling refreshed.
I am becoming healthier and healthier.
All my organs and all parts of my body are working in perfect harmony.
All negative side effects from chemo and/or other medical treatments now leave my body, never to return.
I am pain-free and peaceful.
All negative fear and worry now leave my body.
I am safe and secure.
I love, accept, respect and approve of myself, just as I am.

One of my personal voice recordings

I, Anne Marie Evers, deserve to be and now am becoming healthier and healthier. Negative thoughts of worry and stress now leave my body. My medical reports are healthy and normal.

The negative side effects of the chemotherapy are now disappearing completely: My blood pressure is becoming normal and healthy. I swallow easily and effortlessly. I think clearly now and easily remember the things I need to. I have and enjoy normal healthy circulation in my limbs and entire body. My stomach and intestinal area are calm and peaceful.

I forgive everyone and everything that has ever hurt me. I forgive myself and my health diagnosis. I am healthy, fulfilled, happy, peaceful and prosperous. I love, respect and approve of myself just the way I am. My heart is healing and my grief is 1% less today than it was yesterday. I appreciate my life and my wonderful memories and happy times with Reg 1% more than I did yesterday. I enjoy living in the now.

Thank you, thank you, thank you for the blessings that I have received and am about to receive.

Thank you for this wonderful day.

Affirmations when properly done always work!
(although not always within our preferred time frame or the way we think they should work)

My own healing journey

On 14 July 2013, my life changed forever. One evening, as I was sitting in my chair, I experienced extreme abdominal pain that came about every fifteen minutes. The pain and discomfort were very similar to giving birth to my two children. I also experienced a severe heartburn.

I said to my husband Reggie, "I have to go to the hospital. I am in terrible pain!" He was aware of how anxious I was about seeing doctors and hospitals so he knew it had to be serious for me to ask him to take me there. At Emergency, they examined me and gave me several tests and said that I needed to have surgery immediately. So I did not have much time to prepare (my affirmations), but I quickly started affirming that the surgery was a success and that I recovered quickly.

My angels were on duty

Together with my affirmations for successful surgery, I was asking God and His angels (in whom I personally believe) to help me get through the surgery and to help me accept and handle it. When I was being wheeled into the operating room, I heard a voice in my head very clearly saying the following words: "What time is it?" The loud and clear answer that came back was: "The time is 11:11." I believe that those numbers represent the presence of angels. So I said, "Angels, if you are here to take me home, I am ready, but I would like to have some more time on the planet to be with my family and friends and to help more people." If the answer had been any other of the fifty-nine minutes in the hour, I would not have thought anything about it, but it was the 11:11 that got my attention, as I strongly believe this to be the precise time of angel visitations.

Surgery complete

When the doctors performed emergency surgery, they took out a huge growth that was blocking my colon. They sent it out for biopsy and it came back with the diagnosis of colon cancer. Dr Fry, the operating surgeon, said they got it all. He also said that some of it went into my fat wall and they were able to remove that. (So thank goodness for some fat!)

Waking up in the recovery room

When I came to, I felt like 'the bionic woman'. I had a stint down my throat and was being fed intravenously (hooked up to a machine). I also had one tube for urine, another tube for bowel movements, and oxygen going into my nostrils. I was very uncomfortable, really scared and in pain. The first thought that came into my mind was that I am a strong person and I would get through this. I started visualizing the end result of becoming healthier and healthier.

The affirmation that I was doing—"My surgery is very successful and I recover easily"—turned out to be true! Dr Fry said to me on two occasions, "You are amazing to come through this surgery like you did at your age."

Back to my affirming

I visualized myself healing quickly, completely and easily and used one of my Affirmation Life Tools, the 'Borrow Back' exercise, which worked very well for me. I brought to mind a vivid, colourful picture of myself feeling strong and healthy, speaking at one of my lectures. I 'borrowed back' every single detail—the clothes I was wearing, and how my hair was done, my shoes and jewellery, not leaving out a single detail. I transported that vivid, specific and colourful memory into the present, where I was lying in the hospital bed. I felt as if it was really taking place. I know that the subconscious mind does not know the difference between the real and the unreal, between the seen and the unseen, and just takes us at our word, creating conditions to manifest what we assert and affirm.

Every time I felt uncomfortable, I willed myself to slip into the memory of that wonderful, happy, healthy time in my life and it worked miracles for me. When, in my mind, I put myself into that situation, it made me feel more peaceful, relaxed and hopeful. We should never underestimate the power of the mind and properly done affirmations!

Visualization

I went a step further and visualized myself walking up and down the hospital hallways, getting my exercise. Very soon, I was doing just that! Sometimes, I peeked into a room where a patient looked as if he or she were in distress and I sent them the same message of healing that I was sending to myself. I noticed some of the people that I passed in the hallway (nurses, other patients, visitors) looking at me rather strangely and they probably thought I was talking to myself. I kept on doing my affirmations, walking and sending out love and healing to myself and to everyone I met.

Time to go a step further

I started visualizing myself in vivid, colourful pictures, feeling stronger and stronger, and I saw myself being discharged from the hospital and going home. Then I visualized myself getting out of the car at my home, walking up the steps, going into the living room and sitting down in my favourite chair. I made these visualizations very clear and created them over and over in my mind. At this time, I was saying the following affirmation numerous times daily: "I am perfect, strong, powerful, loving, healthy and happy!" I created another short-form affirmation, saying: "Healthier and healthier ME—NOW!" (It's important to make this statement personal by adding the words, 'me', and you can give it more urgency by adding 'now!')

Some wonderful blessings

Members of my family were there with me every single day and stayed with me. Also some of my friends visited me and did Reiki treatments, meditations, gentle reflexology and more. I received so many cards and flowers that my husband Reggie jokingly said that he might have to rent a truck to take them home. I came to the realization that 'I was too blessed to be stressed!' Dr Fry was pleased with my progress and told me I could go home. I was so excited as I had visualized that trip so many times in my mind. Now that it was actually coming to pass, I kept affirming, "Thank you for abundant health in my body, right here and right now! I am becoming healthier and healthier."

Getting my staples removed

I was home for about five or six days and then went to a local medical clinic to have my staples removed. When I arrived home, I was not feeling great, but then I had just undergone major surgery, so I felt it was probably due to that. I started getting ready to go to a wedding shower for my niece, Kimberley, who was getting married.

I went into the bathroom and everything started running down my legs—and I mean *everything*! When I sat down on the toilet, it was as if my whole body were emptying into the bowl. I called my sister, Darlene, a retired nurse who was visiting us for a few days. She took one look at me and said, "I'll call an ambulance! You have to go to Emergency, now!"

Severe infection: the nightmare that lasted 11 days

I was re-admitted to Lions Gate Hospital about a week or so after my surgery. The nurses had great difficulty finding a vein for the intravenous drip they were trying to place in my arm, and they also had trouble finding my pulse. They took several more tests. My stress level kept rising!

When I was in the Observation Room, I received a blood transfusion. One of the nurses told me later that I was in such bad shape that she was afraid I wouldn't make it, so she prayed for me. I was so thankful that I later gave her a copy of my first book, *Affirmations: Your Passport to Happiness*.

At home, finally...

Because my husband Reggie had also had surgery and could not drive me to my medical appointments, a nurse came to my home to dress my wounds. This was very interesting as I got to tell many of the nurses about the power of affirmations and gave some of them my affirmation books.

I learned the importance of being very specific

I was doing the following affirmation: "My wounds heal quickly and easily." (I had two wounds—one that was healing nicely and a deeper one that was taking longer.) I repeated this affirmation over and over many times during the day. Then, one day, the nurse said to me, "Your wounds are healing very quickly." The way she said it made me question her. I said, "That's good, isn't it?" She replied, "Yes, it's good and not so good because they really need to heal from the inside out—not just on the outside."

This brought clearly to my attention how important it is to be specific when creating and doing affirmations. You must say exactly what you desire. Your subconscious mind takes you at your word and acts accordingly. So I re-worded my affirmation, as follows: "My wounds are healing completely, quickly and easily, from the inside out!" Then the complete healing began. I had many appointments at the Surgical Clinic to have my wound dressings changed, and that lasted for many months. Oh, how I dreaded those appointments. But I did meet some wonderful nurses, doctors and others on my journey.

I asked for a sign

I went to the chemo clinic to have Dr Sasha Smiljanic and Rosemary Hill (wound specialist) look at my wounds to see if they had healed enough for me to start chemotherapy treatments. I was very nervous and repeatedly did affirmations to get rid of fear and calm myself down. I affirmed that my wounds were completely healed. As I had been getting some negative comments about chemo from some people, I asked for a sign as to whether or not I should take chemotherapy. The sign I was looking for was something that would indicate to me that both wounds would be completely healed by 30 September, and that I should then start chemo treatments on 1 October 2013. Both Dr Sasha Smiljanic and Rosemary Hill said those very same words to me, providing the sign that I had asked for! So I went ahead with my plan.

Preventive chemo treatment started on 1 October 2013

My particular six-month chemo treatment consisted of taking two drugs— one orally and the other one intravenously at the hospital every three weeks. I took 6 chemo pills by mouth daily—3 with breakfast and 3 with dinner. I also had to take anti-nausea drugs numerous times during the day for the first few days after the intravenous treatment.

The briefing

Reggie, my daughter Aren and I were briefed on the side effects (of course, they had to share with us the worst-case scenario), and it was overwhelming and very scary. The doctor said it was totally up to me to make the decision, but if I decided not to go for the chemo treatment and the cancer spread (as maybe not all of the cancer had been completely removed), then there would be nothing further they could do for me.

He also said it was not like signing up for a cell phone contract that you cannot get out of and he added that there were no guarantees. He said that they would monitor very closely what was taking place in my body and, if the treatments were too harsh, they would modify them or stop them completely. What a lot of information for anyone to digest!

My decision

It was there and then that I made a commitment to use my Affirmation Life Tools during my chemo treatments and report on how they worked for me. If they were successful for me, I would write a book entitled *Affirmation Life Tools: powerful tools to help with illness and to alleviate the effects of chemotherapy and other medical treatments,* to give hope to others who were undergoing similar treatments. It is my goal to make this information available for cancer patients who are going through the briefing session so they leave that session with a degree of hope. I also intend to make it available to anyone who needs it.

I used my Affirmation Life Tools to help me cope with the negative side effects of the chemotherapy. I found some of the side effects of the drugs to be very disturbing, as many people do. The affirmations did not always make those negative side effects go away, but they did make a *positive* difference in my life and kept me going even when I was tempted to stop taking the chemo treatments.

Before taking any chemo pills

I held the chemo pills in my hand, looked at them and said with great feeling: "I send you love, I bless you, and I thank you for the wonderful treatment you are giving my body today and for going to the right places and working harmoniously with every part of my body, for my highest good, making me cancer-free and abundantly healthy. Thank you, thank you, thank you."

Before taking the intravenous treatment at the hospital

To the chemo drug that I was being given intravenously, I said: "I send you love, I bless you, and I thank you for going to the right places in my body and working harmoniously with every part of my body, for my highest good, making me well and strong. This treatment works well and I am comfortable and at ease. Thank you, thank you, thank you."

My vision

One evening, when I was lying in bed, I said, "Dear God, please give me a sign that I will get through all this and will be able to teach more people about the power of affirmations and Affirmation Life Tools and how helpful they are to people who are coping with health challenges."

I closed my eyes and said, "Thank you, thank you, thank you for the sign." A couple of minutes later, I opened my eyes and looked up into the sky. From my bed, I could see the sky when lying down. All of a sudden, a disk appeared. It was bright and shiny and kept rotating. I watched it for several seconds wondering what it was. Then I saw bright, strong rays of light streaming down to Earth and a wonderful feeling of relief, peace, joy and happiness engulfed me. The picture quickly changed to a huge angel that filled the whole sky and then disappeared. I felt very blessed, peaceful and secure in the knowledge that I was being taken care of and that I would come through this serious health challenge and live my dream of teaching others worldwide the power of my Affirmation Life Tools.

Some of the side effects I experienced

My hands and fingers were ice-cold, tingling and painful; my feet were also ice-cold, swollen, tingling, hurting and my toes felt as if they were fused together. I had a sick stomach, loss of energy, trouble swallowing, very real fear, mouth sores, dry mouth, constipation, trouble focusing my eyes, dizziness, trouble picking things up, sensitivity and blood pressure issues. I felt nauseated, overwhelmed and I lost some of my hair. I was tired and had trouble walking and hearing, at times. After the intravenous treatments at the hospital, I could not write or type. I used my Affirmation Life Tools over and over, affirming healthy and normal functioning of my hands and fingers. Slowly, that ability and my energy came back, for which I was very thankful. I think I had most of the side effects and even more than the ones mentioned above. On several occasions, I woke up feeling like I had a tight bandage on my finger (and I did not have a bandage). I also suffered from nightmares and, at times, woke up in a sweat, shaking and scared.

Fear was my biggest challenge

I have to admit that fear was my constant companion when contemplating the intravenous chemo treatments—and it is still there, to some extent, today. I did not sleep well and I kept waking up and wondering and worrying... *What will it be like? How will my body respond to having poison put into it? Will my body reject the chemo? Will my body work with the chemo? How will I be able to talk, walk and function?* The questions and worries were endless.

The power of words

This made me think of the power of words—the words we speak or the words that are spoken to us—and to remember that we create with every word we speak. Words can uplift, help and raise us up or they can drag us down into a pit of despair. So I decided, right there and then, to take a look at what I was thinking and saying. I did the 'Thought-watching' exercise.

In a small notebook, I made four columns, with the following headings:

Same as yesterday   **Negative**   **Positive**   **New**

For about three days, I watched and listened to my thoughts and words and put a small check mark under the appropriate columns. I thought I was a positive person, but I soon discovered that I was harbouring a lot of negative thoughts, especially about my health situation. And some of the words that I was using were not in my best interests. Only I have the power to eliminate them (after all, I created them in the first place) and to replace them with wonderful, uplifting, happy, joyful, positive thoughts and words.

I asked myself the following questions:

How many negative, self-sabotaging thoughts am I harbouring? How many of them have already taken up residency or are trying to do so in my body, mind and spirit? What am I going to do about it?

I decided that I would replace my negative thoughts with new, positive, happy thoughts of becoming healthier and healthier. So I created new thoughts about how I could handle this challenging situation and get through it. It would not be productive if I was feeling sorry for myself. It would take work, faith, persistence and dedication, but when I reflected on my affirmation teachings, I knew I had to be more diligent in practising what I preached.

Back to the Affirmation Toolbox for help

I developed the following affirmation for dealing with my fears and negative thoughts about my health.

My personal master affirmation for health

I, Anne Marie Evers, deserve to be and now am healthy and happy. My life is full, rich and rewarding. I live in the now. Any and all negative, unwanted fear now leaves my body, never to return, and I am becoming radiantly healthy, right here and right now. I enjoy being calm, peaceful and phobia-free. I thank God daily for all my blessings—the ones I have received, the ones I am receiving and the ones I am about to receive. I am happy and healthy, to the good of all. Thank you, thank you, thank you.
I fully accept.

Signed_____Dated_____
          Anne Marie Evers   *NOW*

My new job

I started reading and studying the information about chemotherapy that I had been given at the hospital. I started browsing the Internet and other places to find out what I could about this process and the side effects. This gave my mind something tangible and practical upon which to focus and I felt I was doing something positive for my health.

A personal tragedy really tested my faith

On 12 December 2013, my beloved husband Reggie passed away in his sleep, in our bed. This was a terrible shock to me as Reggie had been my soul mate and loving husband for seven wonderful, happy years. This happened during the course of my chemo treatments and nothing could have been more traumatic or distressing. My strong faith, my daily practice of affirmations and using my Affirmation Life Tools kept me going. When people ask me how I keep on hosting my weekly radio/Internet talk shows, counselling people, giving workshops and more, I say: "I put one foot in front of the other and keep going." Of course, my affirmations help hugely, and I'm not sure how I would manage without them. It is thanks to the healing effect of these tools that I have been able to resume my life and my work, and to organize additional events, such as my monthly lectures at the local hospital.

If you feel like quitting, it's time for an attitude adjustment!

One evening, when I was coming close to the end of the chemo treatments, I looked at the chemo pills and thought to myself: *I do not want to take you any more. You make me feel lousy. No one will know if I do not take these pills.* Then I felt panic and an urge to run away. But run away to where? To the end of the block and back? I looked outside and it was dark, raining and cold. I realized I would be taking my fears and negativity with me, and running away wouldn't change that. So I had a serious talk with myself.

I said: "Hey, Anne Marie Evers! Listen up! You teach others not to give up, so why not notify yourself to do the same? You need to practise what you preach!" So I took the chemo pills in my hand, looked down at them and said: "Okay. Attitude adjustment time!" And I repeated my earlier affirmation: "I send you love, I bless you and I thank you for going to the right places in my body and working harmoniously with every part of my body, for my highest good, making me cancer-free and healthy. Thank you, thank you, thank you."

I mustered up as much courage and energy as I could and kept going until I actually felt gratitude for the pills and the chemo treatment. I started to experience a form of love as I repeated my affirmation. Emotion that was very close to the surface overtook me and I started sobbing uncontrollably. So I used another affirmation: 'This too shall pass'—and it did! And I am here today writing this book for you and feeling a great deal of gratitude for all my wonderful blessings, in spite of what happened to me.

Fast forward to today

My chemo treatments went on for six months and ended in April 2014. My healing journey has been a long, heartbreaking one, with many stops along the way. Some stops have been interesting, educational and rewarding. I have met many wonderful doctors, nurses and others, and I have been able to share my message of hope and strength with the Affirmation Life Tools that I teach in this book. If I can do it, you certainly can!

Whenever the thought of not taking the chemo drugs surfaced in my mind, I used my powerful 'Cancel, Cancel' affirmation and said, "That negative thought is not true for me." Then I quickly replaced it with a positive, happy one: "I am now becoming healthier and healthier." I kept going and I want to encourage everyone to not give up, and to do what you know deep in your heart is good for you and to follow your wondrous intuition. Family members and others are entitled to their own opinions, but it is YOU and you alone who must make decisions about your body.

Power of the doctor's word

When I first heard the words, "You have colon cancer", I was shocked and thought the doctor was talking about someone else. When those words began to sink in, real fear gripped me and I was on the verge of panic. *Now what? Was this the end?* When the doctor talked about me taking chemo, I was in a daze. Yet, after making it through emergency surgery and a severe infection, here I was, taking the chemo treatments. I wondered, *"Where will it all end?"* It was an intense time of distress, denial, confusion and fear—a rollercoaster of emotions that left me feeling very fragile and vulnerable, yet also feeling lucky to be alive.

Why me?

When a person receives a diagnosis of cancer, his/her reaction may be similar to mine. At first, I felt shock, disbelief and anger. I remember every detail of that conversation and how I reacted when the doctor said those dreaded words. Then I became angry and I asked the most frequently asked question: "Why me?"

Why not you?

When I asked that question, the following resounded in my mind: "Why *not* you? You have a computer; you're a best-selling, published author and writer. You know how to write books. Now is the time to think about writing a book about your health challenge and the things that helped you, such as your Affirmation Life Tools, that would be a help and comfort to others in similar situations!"

Well, that made me sit up and take notice. I thought about it and then I attended a chemo meditation group at the local hospital, where I spoke for a few minutes about the power of affirmations and my Affirmation Life Tools. One woman who had throat cancer and could not speak came up to me afterwards and whispered, "Thank you for coming. You have given me hope." Another participant said, "What are these affirmations you're talking about?" And still another asked if I could show them how to use the Affirmation Life Tools. At that very moment, I made the decision to produce a book, an e-book, an audio book and an e-course about Affirmation Life Tools to help people cope with the side effects of chemo and other medical treatments.

Time to wake up!

Once I accepted the fact that I had colon cancer, I was determined to do whatever I could to get rid of it and to become healthy again. It took several long chats with myself, but I was finally convinced that I needed to focus on what I know best: to do affirmations for healing and whatever else I needed to do to mitigate or resolve this health challenge. I am here today to say to you that you, too, can make affirmations work for you in the most amazing, positive ways. I know it is because of my strong faith, my belief in a higher power, my wonderful, loving, supportive family, my friends and my trusted Affirmation Life Tools that I am well today.

Affirmations when properly done always work!
(although not always within our preferred time frame or the way we think they should work)

PART TWO

Affirmation Life Tools Directory

This book contains 70 tools—30 affirmations and 40 exercises—for coping with the side effects of chemotherapy and other challenging medical treatments, as well as offering support and inspiration for those dealing with career, family, financial and other issues resulting from their health challenges. The following directory lists the various conditions and side effects commonly experienced when undergoing chemo treatments, followed by a list of the various affirmations and exercises.

Note: These Affirmation Life Tools are not designed to stop or eliminate negative side effects (although they often do). Nor are they meant to replace medical intervention, where required. (You are advised to consult your doctor/healthcare practitioner for any health concerns you may have.) These tools have been created and designed to help with the management of the negative side effects you may be experiencing during/after chemotherapy. They are also designed to help you relax your mind and give you something positive and uplifting upon which to focus. Many people say that the use of these Affirmation Life Tools gives them peace, hope and some form of control over their thinking and feeling. These tools can be used for anything in your life that you wish to change, correct or remove. They can be used at any time—not just when you are going through a medical challenge, chemo or other challenging medical treatments.

SIDE EFFECTS

AFFIRMATIONS

EXERCISES

Using the Affirmation Life Tools

Before using the Affirmation Life Tools, please check with your doctor to see if the side effects you are having require immediate medical treatment and then, and only then, use these simple, effective Affirmation Life Tools to help you manage and cope with the side effects.

ANEMIA

1% Solution affirmation

Say this affirmation with great feeling, anticipation and excitement: "I have and continue to have the perfect, healthy iron level for my body. I am 1% stronger and healthier today than I was yesterday." Repeat this statement several times daily.

One of my readers sent me the following e-mail:

When lying in a hospital bed in excruciating pain, with one tube sticking out of my nose and another one out of my belly, I found it very difficult—if not downright impossible—to say, "I am 100% healthy. So I devised a way to have it work for me." I said, "Today, I am 1% better than I was yesterday!" That worked for me because my mind could and did believe that I was 1% better and made it happen.

Note: If your faith is strong enough that you can believe in yourself getting 10% stronger and healthier every day, then say 10% instead of 1%. The important factor to remember here is believability. You must believe that it's at least technically possible for you to get 1–10% healthier every day. Use the percentage that your mind is willing to accept and work with, so it will not cancel out your affirmation.

Another reader shared the following story with me about this affirmation:

I was very intrigued when I heard you speak about the 1% Solution on your radio show. So I tried it. I was very ill in the hospital and I just could not bring myself to say that I was 100% healthy. So I did as you suggested and said: "Today, I am 1% better than I was yesterday." And it worked! I think it was because my subconscious mind could and did believe the 1% but did not believe that I could be 100% better. Wow! What a wonderful method. I will use it again whenever needed. This message should be shared with the world. So many thanks are in order!

Borrow Back exercise

Find a quiet place where you will not be disturbed. Go back in your mind and recall a time in your life when you had a healthy iron level in your body and when you felt strong, healthy and full of life. Make the image very colourful and vivid, bringing in every detail. Perhaps you were playing golf or some other sport. Where were you? What were you wearing? Who was with you? Affix that image securely in your mind. Then mentally transport it into the present moment. Enjoy and allow those feelings of complete health and happiness to saturate every cell and every part of your body as you receive this vibrant energy. Your subconscious mind does not differentiate between a real and an imaged event, and you can use this to your benefit, every time you visualize.

Engage your five physical senses:

See yourself becoming healthy, strong and happy.
Hear people commenting on how healthy you look.
Feel happy, relaxed and content.
Smell your favourite scent of essential oil, perfume or cologne.
Taste some fresh sparkling water or visualize biting into a juicy apple.

Use your own voice recording

Listen to the recording you created with your own voice. When you listen to it every single night, you are allowing the message to sink deep into your subconscious mind, where it can take root, grow and manifest your desire. Wake up feeling great, trusting that the iron level in your body is normalizing and your strength and vitality are returning!

Message from your affirmation life coach

Feel the energy and strength flowing throughout your body. You are becoming stronger and healthier. You have taken the first step on your wonderful health journey. I am in your cheering section, every step of the way.

Affirmations when properly done always work!
(although not always within our preferred time frame or the way we think they should work)

APPETITE LOSS

Bless Your Food exercise

Before eating and taking your chemo pills and/or intravenous treatment, close your eyes and bless your food, chemo pills, beverages and chemo treatment. Instruct your food, beverages and chemo treatments to go to the right places in your bod
y and work harmoniously, bringing strength, healing and nourishment. Make a sincere effort to eat and drink slowly. Eat small meals throughout the day. Avoid sweets and fried or fatty foods, and make sure you have plenty of water and other fluids. Limit your caffeine intake and follow the hospital dietician's advice as much as possible.

Note: I found it very helpful to eat slower and to focus on my food going to the right places in my body, for my highest good. I was very careful to wash my hands frequently, and always before eating. I drank lots of fluids and exercised a little each day. Every single thing helped in some small way.

The Next Time affirmation

When I felt that I had not eaten enough food or healthy food at a meal, I used my 'Next Time' affirmation. Instead of beating myself up and saying, "I should have eaten more healthy food," I said, "Cancel, cancel. That is in the past and the next time I will do it differently." And I did! This affirmation can be used for any situation in your life when you want to avoid any feelings of guilt or self-reproach.

Healthy Eating visualization

When I completely lost my appetite and experienced difficulty even thinking about eating, I decided it was time to do something about it. First, I had a serious talk with myself. I told myself that if I did not eat healthy, nutritious food, my body would not be able to heal.

In my mind, I visualized in vivid colour an excellent chef, complete with chef's hat, preparing a delicious meal for me. (My first husband was a famous chef, so this visualization was very easy for me to do.) I watched, in my mind, as he lovingly prepared the vegetables, fruit and other healthy food. Then he took one of my best plates from my cabinet and arranged the food beautifully on it. He put on some soft, background music and handed me a glass of sparkling mineral water. I felt so loved and cared for as we sat down and ate this delicious food. I savoured every mouthful. It was so special. I was amazed that the metallic taste in my mouth, which I had been struggling with for some time, just sort of faded into the background and I actually could taste the wonderful flavours of the food. Every time I did not want to eat, I just found a comfortable place to sit and did this meditation in my mind. Then I got up and prepared similar food for me to actually eat. I changed my visualization from time to time but it was always special. Most importantly of all, it worked!

Say often to yourself: "I am hungry for healthy, nutritious food and I enjoy eating." Never underestimate the power of your words and your subconscious mind.

Dr Bernie Siegel shared the following story with me when he was a guest on one of my radio shows. He said he told his patients before surgery that they would wake up hungry and thirsty. Then he started getting complaints that his patients were gaining weight. So he changed his statement to: "You will wake up hungry but you won't finish everything on your plate." ...and the complaints stopped coming. Such is the power of our subconscious mind.

Use your own voice recording

Listen to your positive recording every night and wake up feeling great, trusting that your appetite is becoming completely normal and that you are eating the right amount of healthy and nourishing food for your body's highest good.

Message from your affirmation coach

Feel your appetite returning. Did you bless your food, today? You are on the right track! Congratulations!

Affirmations when properly done always work!
(although not always within our preferred time frame or the way we think they should work)

BLOOD PRESSURE ISSUES

When I had a challenge with my blood pressure, I used the following tools.

Step Ahead in Your Mind exercise

Step ahead in your mind and visualize yourself in some future place or state of mind that has not yet taken place. Put yourself into the picture, creating vivid, colourful mental images of you having normal, healthy blood pressure and it staying that way. Practise deep breathing. Say, "Cancel, cancel" to any negative thoughts, fears and worry. Say, "I deserve and now have, and continue to have, normal blood pressure."

Flashlight exercise

This is one of my favourite Affirmation Life Tools. I took a black or green felt-tip pen and wrote on a piece of card paper, in huge letters, NORMAL, HEALTHY BLOOD PRESSURE, ME, NOW! I put the paper and a flashlight in my bathroom, where it was dark. When I got up in the middle of the night to use the bathroom, I aimed my flashlight at the paper and switched it on and off three times, while focusing on those words. I repeated this process three times. Then I went back to bed and immediately feel asleep again. This type of programming flashes the images into your brain and the turning off and on of the light reinforces the message of what you want your brain to see and remember. It is a very powerful and effective process.

Blood Pressure visualization exercise

Visualize in your mind's eye being on a warm, sandy beach. You are watching the gentle waves caress the shore. Feel the warm breeze wafting over your body, keeping your temperature perfect. You are enjoying every single moment. You can feel your blood pressure becoming normal and healthy. As you take several deep breaths, breathing in health and happiness, feel how great it is not to have to worry about your blood pressure. It is normalizing and you are becoming calmer and calmer.

Engage your five physical senses

See the numbers you wish your blood pressure to be on your doctor's machine.
Hear your doctor saying, "Your blood pressure is normal!"

Feel how calm and relaxed you are.

Smell your favourite flower scent, perfume and/or cologne.

Taste some fresh sparkling water or visualize biting into a juicy apple.

Breathing IN/OUT exercise

Find a place to relax where you will not be disturbed. Clear your mind of all thoughts and worries. Take a couple of deep breaths, breathing OUT fear, worry and any negativity, and breathing IN peace, joy, healthy normal blood pressure and happiness. Breathe in to the count of four, hold for the count of seven and then breathe out to the count of eight. Repeat this exercise as often as needed.

Use your own voice recording

Listen to your own voice recording every night and wake up trusting that your blood pressure is becoming completely normal!

Message from your affirmation life coach

You are on the right track—and it shows. Your doctor/healthcare practitioner will be very pleased with your normal blood pressure readings. Great stuff!

Affirmations when properly done always work!
(although not always within our preferred time frame or the way we think they should work)

BRAIN (CHEMO) FOG

Brain (chemo) fog is a commonly used term that sums up feelings of confusion, forgetfulness, lack of focus and mental clarity. You feel as if you *just can't think*, which can be very frustrating. Everyone feels a little fuzzyheaded, at times, but if you frequently suffer from brain fog, it is important to work at restoring your mental clarity. When I realized this was what was happening to me, I decided I needed to do something about it, and I used the following tools, with great success.

Clear, Search and Retrieve exercise

When you wish to remember an incident, situation, person's name, answers for an exam etc, use the Clear Search and Retrieve exercise. Sit quietly, gently close your eyes and totally relax, taking several deep breaths. Say to your mind, "Clear" and visualize and feel your mind becoming clear and relaxed. Then say, "Search" and imagine finding your mental filing cabinet with the many folders it contains. Search for the file folder that has the answer to the question that you wish to remember. Then say, "Retrieve" and mentally see, feel and hear that file being downloaded into your mind. Say, "Thank you, thank you, thank you for the perfect answer." Usually, the answer will flash into your mind in seconds, minutes or hours. At certain times, it may take a little longer—maybe a day or so. Trust this process and know that it always works! Some of the chemo patients at our local hospital are having wonderful success with this particular Affirmation Life Tool and are using it numerous times daily.

When I feel it is difficult to think or to remember things, I know that this is due to mild cognitive impairment and that it, too, shall pass. I use my 'This Too Shall Pass' affirmation many, many times during the day—so much so that it has become my constant mantra.

I know of many others who have also been helped by the 'Clear, Search and Retrieve' exercise. One chemo patient—Anita, a lovely young woman who had breast cancer and was undergoing chemo and radiation treatment—found it particularly effective. We were sitting together on my sun deck, one afternoon, and I noticed that she had paused several times when talking to me, saying she couldn't remember what it was she wanted to say. I suggested she try the 'Clear, Search and Retrieve' exercise. She looked at me and I could tell she was a bit skeptical. But when I explained this process to her, she decided to try it immediately. I watched as she used it three times successfully that afternoon. She later reported using it many times daily with immediate and accurate success, and it has become one of her favourite Affirmation Life Tools.

Pail of Dirty Water exercise

A huge percentage of our bodies is made up of water, which represents emotion. When your brain feels cloudy and murky, do the following powerful exercise. Physically take a small pail and fill it with some dirty water (dishwater or the water you have washed the floor with). Place the pail in the sink, turn on the tap and watch the slow, steady trickle of pure clear water going into the pail. I liken this to the pure, clear, healthy energy and power going into my mind. That murkiness starts to clear and the water eventually becomes completely clear. I liken this process to releasing murky thoughts, fear and negativity from my brain and replacing them with pure, clear, positive and happy thoughts.

When I did this exercise, I found that all negativity and murkiness evaporated. I performed this exercise several times and really did begin to feel better as I had a visual upon which to focus my mind. My mind was becoming clearer and clearer and that nasty brain (chemo) fog began to lift, as if by magic. It is so great to be able to think clearly and quickly and to remember things that I need to remember. I said, "Thank you, thank you, thank you," and carried on with my day.

Use your own voice recording

Listen to your voice recording in bed at night and wake up with a clear, healthy brain/mind. All that brain (chemo) fog has completely lifted and you can now think clearly.

Message from your affirmation life coach

Wow! Look at that bright, healing light coming in through the window and going right into your brain, clearing away any remnants of brain (chemo) fog. You see clearly now that the fog has gone!

Affirmations when properly done always work!
(although not always within our preferred time frame or the way we think they should work)

CHEST AND LUNG CONGESTION

Going, Going, Gone affirmation

When you encounter the negative side effect of feeling as though your chest and lungs are congested, visualize a huge whiteboard with an erasable marker. Picture yourself picking up the marker and writing on the board, 'congestion in my chest and lungs'. Then imagine picking up a blue-coloured marker and writing right over those words, 'Going, going, gone!' Look at those words for a few seconds, take a deep breath and erase everything you have just written, saying to yourself, "My chest and lung congestion is now gone!"

When I used this affirmation, I found that repeating this sentence over and over really helped to ease this condition. I believe our minds are very powerful and, when directed in a specific way, can and do create many wonderful miracles.

Borrow Back exercise

Recall and visualize a time when you had normal healthy breathing and clear chest and lungs. Transport this image into your present moment and visualize your chest and lungs looking clear and healthy and free of any negativity. Say: "I love taking deep breaths that relax me and clear away any congestion in my lungs."

Use your own voice recording

Listen to the audio recording that you created with your own voice and wake up trusting that your chest and lung area are already clearer and healthier. All congestion has completely disappeared.

Message from your affirmation life coach

Be proud of yourself for improving your breathing and clearing your chest and lungs. You are a powerful manifester! Keep up the good work!

Affirmations when properly done always work!
(although not always within our preferred time frame or the way we think they should work)

CONSTIPATION/DIARRHEA

Borrow Back exercise

Recall a time when you had normal, regular bowel movements and how healthy and powerful that felt. See yourself in vivid colour in your mind's eye. Visualize and imagine pure radiant health pouring into your body, saturating every cell and every part of your body. Then just sit quietly and be with it. When you feel you have finished for that particular time, say: "Thank you, thank you, thank you," and trust that things are already improving.

Release of Constipation affirmation

Say: "I allow my body to physically and mentally release old, out-dated ideas, thoughts and negativity. My digestive system is working in perfect order, together with my intestinal tract. All waste and toxins from my digestive system and every part of my body are now released and leave my body immediately. I have and enjoy normal, regular bowel movements." Or: "I gladly release all unwanted waste material from my body now."

Ask for Help from the Creator affirmation

"To the creator who created my body and knows exactly how it works, I thank you for helping me to keep on having normal, regular bowel movements. I ask now that this health process be complete in my body. I now relax and take several deep breaths, breathing out all negativity and breathing in peace, joy and thankfulness for this wondrous miracle now taking place in my body. I live in an attitude of gratitude."

Attitude of Gratitude affirmation

"Thank you, body, for keeping me regular all these years and keeping my insides clean and healthy." Being grateful helps to reduce the stress and worry that may be blocking your regular bowel movements. Affirm: "I deserve and now have normal and regular bowel movements."

Some helpful hints
- Drink some fresh lemon juice and olive oil mixed together in warm water.
- Exercise gently, or as much as you can, as this stimulates the bowel.

- Gently massage your abdomen.
- Eat prunes regularly.
- Drink plenty of pure water.
- If necessary, talk to your doctor about stool softeners and laxatives.
- You may wish to bring some comical or interesting reading material with you into the bathroom.

Use your own voice recording

At bedtime, listen to the audio recording that you created with your own voice and look forward to waking up knowing that today and every day you will be experiencing normal and healthy bowel movements.

Message from your affirmation life coach

Constipation is a thing of the past, for you. Congratulations on releasing and letting go of any old or current negative thoughts and emotions. You are victorious!

Affirmations when properly done always work!
(although not always within our preferred time frame or the way we think they should work)

DEPRESSION

Depression can be an additional factor in a serious illness. One reader, Kenneth, had been suffering from depression and had been prescribed anti-depressants by his doctor. However, he reported doing health and happiness affirmations several times a day for three months, after which he felt so much better that he went to his doctor and asked him to lower the dose of his anti-depressant medication. Kenneth is still doing his affirmations and feeling better and better.

Shower exercise

When you take your daily shower and rub soap over your body, visualize it cleansing every speck of negativity, making your body squeaky-clean. Visualize the cleansing water going down the drain and taking with it your depression and unhappy thoughts. Treat your body with reverence, giving it the proper healthy food and an exercise program that befits your age, health challenges and particular lifestyle.

Whiteboard exercise

Visualize a whiteboard with an erasable marker in front of you. Take the marker and write: 'My depression.' Just beside those words write: 'My depression—going, going, gone!' Now keep a picture of that image in your mind and imagine erasing everything you've just written. Take a deep breath, breathing OUT all pain, depression and/or discomfort. Then breathe IN healing, peace, contentment and joy. Stay with this feeling of complete comfort and happiness for a few minutes, saying to yourself, "Thank you, thank you, thank you," and trusting that your body's excellent healing mechanism is working ideally for you.

Stop Sign exercise

I downloaded from the Internet a coloured picture of a stop sign. I cut the picture out and pasted it on a piece of cardboard. I took a popsicle stick and glued it on to make a handle. I put it by my chair and then made another one for my desk. When a nasty side effect pops up with its companions, fear and depression, I pick up one of the stop signs, look at it and then say very loudly, "Stop!" (I sometimes visualize a flag person at a construction site standing with a stop sign, directing traffic.) At the same time, I snap the elastic band on my wrist (kept there for that purpose) or stamp my foot to anchor that command in my subconscious mind and to re-direct my thinking. I have fun with this exercise and it really works for me. Try it and see what it does for you.

Healing Tree visualization

Visualize a beautiful, big old tree in front of you. **See** the tree in all its character and beauty. **Feel** what it is like when you hug the tree and, as you do, **smell** the wondrous earthy smell of its bark. **Hear** the birds chirping and the gentle breeze caressing your face. **Taste** the fresh, clear, invigorating water in your water container. Now, imagine seeing steps leading up to a door in the trunk of the tree. You open the door and see a big comfortable chair on a soft rug. You go inside and sink deeply into the chair. Enjoy the feeling of peace and relaxation flowing through you. All depression is evaporating. This is your special healing place, where you alone can go to think, create and do your affirmations. Feel your whole body being saturated with Divine healing and know that you are becoming healthier and depression-free. Thank the tree and go on with your day.

You may also wish to find an actual place in nature for doing your affirmations, such as a garden, meadow, tree house, arbour or anywhere you feel comfortable and at peace. Make this your private, sacred place for stillness and healing.

Use your own voice recording

Listen to the audio recording that you created with your own voice and wake up trusting that you are now depression-free. This tool can be used any time you wish.

Message from your affirmation life coach

I am so proud of you. You inspire me! You have made such great progress in becoming happy, balanced and depression-free. These powerful Affirmation Life Tools ARE working miracles in your life!

Affirmations when properly done always work!
(although not always within our preferred time frame or the way we think they should work)

EARACHE, HEARING LOSS AND DISCOMFORT

This Too Shall Pass affirmation

I use this tool many times during the day and whenever I fear that the side effect that I'm experiencing is permanent, I say: "This side effect is temporary," and then say: "This too shall pass"—and it passes! You cannot overuse these five little words. And remember that words have power and you create with every word you speak.

Going, Going, Gone exercise

Think about your ears being plugged—possibly with pain and/or strange noises. Decide in your mind that you are totally releasing these conditions now. Visualize your whiteboard and marker, and write the words in large, bold letters: MY EAR DISCOMFORT. Then visualize writing over those words the following: Going, going, gone! To complete this exercise, visualize yourself erasing everything that you have just written, while taking a deep breath and, on the exhale, imagining those negative conditions dissolving, never to return. Softly whisper, "Thank you, thank you, thank you."

Note: The manifestation of your desire does not always happen immediately. It can take time and requires diligently practising the affirmations and tools with faith, gratitude and expectancy.

Use your own voice recording

Listen to the audio recording that you created with your own voice and wake up trusting that the hearing in both of your ears is now returning to normal.

Message from your affirmation life coach

You are doing such a great job that even you are totally amazed. Keep it up! You are truly a winner in life. You have the gift of healing and clear hearing in both of your ears, starting right now!

Affirmations when properly done always work!
(although not always within our preferred time frame or the way we think they should work)

EXTREMITIES (ARMS)

Pain, restriction and discomfort in my arm

When I came home from the hospital after intravenous chemo treatment, I experienced severe pain and restriction in my arm where the IV had been inserted. Using the following Affirmation Life Tools gave me a certain amount of relief.

Borrow Back exercise

I visualized myself at a time when I was able to move my arm easily, without pain or discomfort. I selected a time when I was very active, playing tennis. I recreated that scene in detail in my mind, being very specific and making the images very colourful and real. I felt as if it were really taking place and I transported that vivid image into my present moment.

Then I said, "Thank you, thank you, thank you," and carried on with my day, feeling wonderful movement in my arm and not a trace of pain. I was so excited and could not wait to share my experience with my family and friends. Whenever I felt any pain or discomfort, I willed myself to bring that vivid memory of that happy time back into my present moment. This exercise helped me to increase my faith and belief in my own healing ability.

This Too Shall Pass affirmation

When I felt pain and restriction in my arm, I said, "Relax, this is not coming from my arm or my body, it is a side effect of the chemo, which is temporary and this too shall pass." I took several deep breaths, breathing OUT fear and panic and breathing IN love, health, healing and peacefulness. Then I began to relax, flexing my fingers, opening and closing them many times and swinging my arms back and forth. Slowly, my body started to respond. I took a deep breath and said, "Thank you, thank you, thank you for my wonderful healing!" Then I sat for a few moments and felt totally present in that feeling of calmness and peace.

Use your own voice recording

Listen to the audio recording that you created with your own voice and wake up feeling happy and excited that you can move your arms, hands and fingers freely and that you are totally pain-free!

Message from your affirmation life coach

You are becoming an expert in using these tools. You have been telling your arm and other parts of your body that these side effects are caused by the chemotherapy and that they are temporary, and your arm is responding nicely. I am impressed with the great job you're doing, despite all these challenges. You deserve a medal!

Affirmations when properly done always work!
(although not always within our preferred time frame or the way we think they should work)

EXTREMITIES (HANDS AND FINGERS)

The side effects of chemotherapy/other medical treatments may include numbness, feeling ice-cold, loss of sensation to heat and cold, loss of strength and a lack of awareness of your extremities. Rub your hands together briskly to get the energy flowing. Ask for healing energy and normal feeling to flow through your hands and fingers, healing, soothing and creating normal, healthy circulation.

This Too Shall Pass affirmation

Hold your hands in front of you, spread out your fingers and say, "Hands and fingers, I love you, I bless you, and I thank you. You have served me well for many years. I know it is not you or my body that is causing this negative side effect of not being able to type, write or grasp things etc. It is a side effect of my chemo treatment, and I know this too shall pass." Tell your hands and fingers that your circulation is becoming perfect and working harmoniously in your body, for your highest good.

Create Movement in Hands and Fingers affirmation

Move your fingers back and forth. Take a pen and write, "I am becoming healthier and healthier." Say to yourself, "I am so thankful that I am able to write this sentence." Then sign and date it. After doing this affirmation, look at what you've written and, with a great feeling of gratitude, say: "Thank you, thank you, thank you, fingers, for writing so easily and smoothly."

When I did this exercise shortly after my intravenous chemo treatment, I kept what I wrote, as a reminder that I was actually able to write this sentence. I have to admit that it was a little difficult to read and it took me much longer to write than usual, but I did it.

Go to your computer and type an e-mail. When you have finished, say, "Thank you, thank you, thank you, fingers, for typing this e-mail. I love you and I bless you." Then live in an attitude of gratitude for this wondrous blessing. Just think how restricting it was to feel that you were unable to write, type and/or do other daily tasks.

Appreciation and gratitude

Think of all the wonderful tasks and things that your hands and fingers have performed, taking care of your family, cooking, washing, driving, doing household tasks, and wiping away tears when your child skinned his or her knee, or placing your hand on your child's forehead when your child had a fever. Think of all the typing, computer work, writing and other important work your fingers did for you—things you perhaps took for granted. Now, feel deep love and appreciation flow from your heart into your hands and fingers, bringing back the feeling and keeping them warm and healthy. Then wrap your hands in a warm heating pad, in a hot towel or around a hot water bottle

Since doing this simple exercise, I've looked very differently at my hands and fingers and no longer take them for granted. I appreciate and thank them every day. Think about it. How many times in your life have you stopped to appreciate and thank your hands and fingers for their loving support and wonderful work?

Other things that may help

- Use a heating pad for your arms, hands and fingers to keep them warm.
- Be careful not to pick up very hot or very cold items.
- Gently massage your hands, arms and feet to stimulate circulation and help clear toxins from your extremities.
- Rest your body and get lots of sleep.
- Wear warm socks and/or gloves.
- When cutting up vegetables or anything else, look at your hands when cutting, so you don't injure yourself.
- Check the temperature of the water you're using to make sure it's not too hot. You can put your elbow into the water or use a thermometer in your bath water, for example.

Extremities and Peripheral Neuropathy affirmation

Hold your hands in front of you with your fingers spread out and say the following affirmation:

Master affirmation for increased circulation

All my extremities are now working normally. My hands and fingers are becoming warm and enjoying normal, healthy circulation. I say to my hands and fingers: "You have served me well for all these years. I love you, I bless you, and I thank you. It is now easy for me to type, write, cook and do all the other things that allow me to carry on with my life normally and effortlessly. This side effect is not from you or any part of my body; it is one of the negative side effects of chemotherapy. It is temporary and this too shall pass. I am becoming radiantly healthy, happy and peaceful, to the good of all parties concerned. Thank you, thank you, thank you.

I fully accept.

Signed_____Dated_____

Use your own voice recording

Listen to the audio recording that you created with your own voice and wake up feeling happy and excited about the total flexibility and normal feeling in your hands and fingers.

Message from your affirmation life coach

I am so excited for you. Can you feel that strength, feeling and circulation flowing into your hands and fingers, making them healthy and normal? I am totally amazed at your wonderful progress. Keep up the good work!

Affirmations when properly done always work!
(although not always within our preferred time frame or the way we think they should work)

EXTREMITIES (LEGS AND FEET)

When my feet were ice-cold, swelling, tingling and hurting, and my toes felt as if they were fused together, I used the following Affirmation Life Tools.

Gratitude for My Legs and Feet affirmation

Gently place your hands and fingers on your legs and feet, saying: "My legs and feet are now becoming healthier and healthier and I enjoy unrestricted movement and freedom from pain and swelling. I have normal circulation throughout my limbs and my body. I feel the healing energy saturating my entire being, making me completely whole and healthy." Spend a few minutes with your eyes closed, enjoying the wonderful healing and visualizing the soothing energy doing its job in a perfect way. You are so grateful. When you feel complete, slowly open your eyes and trust that healing is already underway.

Oil of oregano foot soak and massage

I soaked my feet in warm water with a few drops of oil of oregano and kept my feet elevated as much as possible. I also purchased a U-comfy Leg and Foot Massager to increase circulation. If you are not in a position to purchase the machine, use a tennis ball or foot roller and exercise your feet by rolling them over the ball/roller. You will be massaging the reflexology points and promoting circulation by giving your feet a workout.

Foot-massage affirmation

You might also apply some soothing/healing cream or essential oil to your feet, and massage each one in turn, saying: "Dear foot, you have served me well for many years, for which I thank you and bless you, and I now ask that you return to your normal healthy condition so I can walk easily and effortlessly without any pain or discomfort. I have and enjoy perfect circulation in my legs, ankles, feet, toes and every part of my body. Thank you, thank you, thank you."

Anchor Good Feelings exercise

Anchor feelings of your feet and toes being healthy, strong and pain-free. Do this by visualizing your feet as completely healthy and enjoying perfect circulation. When you get the feeling of faith and excitement, then gently touch each foot and anchor that wonderful feeling to them. Be kind and loving to your feet and they will respond accordingly.

Do you feel you need some comfort in your life? Go back in your mind to when you were a child and were playing in the mud or on the sand at the beach. Feel how it felt on your bare feet when you walked and played in the mud/sand. Bring that warm, wet and soothing experience of swishing your toes and feet in that mud/sand. Think about how safe, happy and relaxed you were. Bring that memory back in vivid detail into your present moment and re-experience it with all the sensations you felt at that time.

Master affirmation for healthy feet

I, [your name], deserve and now have normal, healthy circulation and conditions in my feet and whole body. I lovingly take care of my feet and they serve me well. All swelling in my ankles and feet is now gone and I enjoy walking, running, dancing and other physical activities. My feet are becoming healthier and healthier and pain-free. I am happy and healthy, to the good of all parties concerned. Thank you, thank you, thank you.

I fully accept.

*Signed*_____*Dated*_____

When you are satisfied that you are taking proper care of your feet, act as if they are already completely healed and healthy. When walking, whisper: "Thank you, thank you, thank you for my healthy legs, feet and whole body."

Use your own voice recording

Listen to the audio recording that you created with your own voice and wake up feeling happy and excited about having healthy circulation in your legs, feet and whole body.

Message from your affirmation life coach

Gratitude and self-talk have been your constant companions on this health journey and now they are paying off for you, big time. Feel that perfect circulation and pain-free movement of your legs, ankles and feet. You have done an excellent job and you are now reaping the benefits. You are the greatest! Keep going!

Affirmations when properly done always work!
(although not always within our preferred time frame or the way we think they should work)

EYES (FOCUSING ISSUES/DISCOMFORT)

When I experience difficulty focusing my eyes, I use the following Affirmation Life Tools to help me cope.

Binocular exercise

I pick up my binoculars (opera glasses) and focus my eyes easily and effortlessly on something beautiful—such as the flowers in my garden or a painting or a photo somewhere in my home. I engage my five physical senses, imagining myself seeing clearly and distinctly, hearing people commenting on my excellent vision, feeling so happy being able to see everything clearly and distinctly, smelling my favourite flower scent, and enjoying the taste of a juicy apple. Now, whenever I have the side effect of not being able to focus or see clearly, I immediately bring to mind these wonderful vivid images.

Near and Far Vision exercise

Hold one of your fingers in front of your eyes. Focus for a few seconds on that finger then look away to a far-away object, such as a tree in the distance. Now, focus on that object for several seconds and then go back to focusing on your finger. Do this exercise several times, going back and forth between objects near and far. Repeat as many times a day as you wish. Then relax and enjoy your improved eyesight.

Health Garden exercise

Before preparing your Health Garden, clear your mind and put yourself in a positive, receptive mode. Make sure that your heart and mind are in agreement, and then do the following five-step process.

1. Prepare the soil. Prepare the fertile soil of your subconscious mind by forgiving everyone and everything that has ever hurt you. You may wish to forgive yourself for not taking better care of your eyes or for not being more proactive and diligent with your health.

2. Select the seed you desire. Decide exactly what you want. Be very specific. Focus on your eyes becoming clearer and healthier. Clear your mind of all fears and concentrate on healing and living life to the fullest. Then create your master affirmation.

3. Water and fertilize. Take out your master affirmation every morning and evening and read it over, knowing that your subconscious mind is taking in every detail and storing it for all time. All those positive words of healing and health are sinking deep into your subconscious mind, where they can take root and serve to manifest your desire.

4. Anticipate the harvest. Mentally see yourself accepting the desired outcome: perfect eyesight, 20/20 vision. Engage your five senses. **See** everything clearly; **hear** people commenting on how your eyesight has improved; **feel** how your eyes are focusing perfectly; **smell** your favourite flower fragrance; and, for **taste**, visualize biting into a juicy apple.

5. Take delivery. Accept that wondrous healing power and abundant health. Know that you already are becoming healthier, and allow yourself to embody a feeling of relief and gratitude for the gift of your wonderful eyes.

Use your own voice recording

Listen to the audio recording that you created with your own voice and wake up trusting that your vision and focus are already improving.

Message from your affirmation life coach

It's so inspiring for me to see the progress you're making, using these powerful Affirmation Life Tools! It sure feels good to see clearly and to have some control over the focusing process, doesn't it? Congratulations from your cheerleader!

Affirmations when properly done always work!
(although not always within our preferred time frame or the way we think they should work)

FATIGUE AND STRESS

Cup-emptying exercise

Take one of your cups and, on masking tape with a felt-tip pen, write: 'My excessive fatigue and stress.' Place the masking tape on the cup. Fill the cup with water, sit down with it in your hands and visualize all your fatigue and stress dripping into the cup—from your eyes, ears, nose and mouth. Feel all negativity leaving your body. Stay with it until you feel that you have released as much as you can, then take the cup to the sink and dump the water down the drain, knowing that you can never get that water back and with it has gone your fatigue, stress and worry. Then, imagine filling up that empty space you just created with positive, happy, healthy, healing energy, trusting that all that negative stress and fatigue has left your body.

I personally found this tool very helpful. When I do this exercise, I can feel the fatigue and worry disappearing from my body, to be replaced by an overall sense of calm and peace.

Note: You can do the above exercise and focus on just releasing fatigue. When the exercise is complete, say: "Thank you, thank you, thank you for helping me release that tiredness completely," and then add the words, "I am energized, invigorated, rejuvenated and excited about doing all the things I wish to accomplish today."

For best results, perform this exercise for 21 consecutive days, as it takes that long to create a new habit. Never underestimate the power of your mind to heal your own body.

Ellen, one of my readers, shared with me the following story of forgiveness and asked me to share it with you.

When I was diagnosed with cancer and was being treated, my husband George had an affair. He confessed and vowed it would never happen again. I was so angry with him. I could not imagine how he could cheat on me when I was fighting for my life. I became obsessed with rage. A friend gifted me with a copy of your Affirmations Book and I started reading. The part about forgiveness intrigued me. I took a cup that had his name on it, filled it with water, sat down with the cup in my hands and visualized my rage, anger and hurt dripping from my eyes, ears, nose and mouth and going into the water.

When I went to take it to the sink to dump the water down the drain, I was shocked! It is hard to describe what happened. The cup with the water in it was so heavy that I literally had to take two hands to carry it to the sink! I swear it weighed 10 pounds! I continued doing this exercise (sometimes several times during the day) and the ice around my heart started to melt. I started feeling more loving toward George. Now, I could even look at him without anger. We had long, serious talks about the situation and I decided to forgive my husband. He said that he thought I was dying and was overcome with grief. I know that is not an excuse, but there and then I decided to work on making our marriage solid. We are both working on rebuilding our love relationship on a solid foundation of loving kindness, forgiveness and understanding. We are taking it one day at a time and, now, a year later, we are still together. Our hearts are full of gratitude to you for sharing such a simple process that worked a miracle for us. We cannot thank you enough!

Another reader, Louise (a teacher from Rhode Island), shared her experience of using this exercise:

I always knew, deep down inside, that I was a good person, but it was hard for me to bring that positive feeling to the surface of my mind. I did this by doing the cup-emptying exercise that you teach. I poured out all the negative feelings that were sitting on top of my positive knowingness and success. Now, my feelings of self-worth, self-love and respect are surfacing. I am so delighted! I'm doing better in every respect of my life and am so grateful for you and your writings.

Write it Out exercise

Make a list of everything you are stressed about. List even what you may think are silly things. Then date and sign it, place it in a drawer and leave it there for six months or so. Then, take it out and read it and you will be amazed to discover that the things you were stressed about somehow worked out better than you ever imagined.

Then ask yourself, "Why am I wasting my precious time being stressed?" When you write it down on paper you are transferring it to a real object (piece of paper) and, on some level, letting it go.

A practical step you can take

In your local area, check out the relaxation programs in the outpatient oncology clinics that offer help and support. They can play an important role in managing pain and side effects.

Feeling deeply fatigued can be due to a number of factors:

- worry and stress—a huge issue, for many of us
- the cancer itself
- worry about how the diagnosis has affected or will affect our spouse and/or children
- treatment of the disease and finding the best solution
- the emotional aspects of coping with cancer and all its symptoms
- financial concerns due to medical costs and/or not being able to work.

Tips to help you reduce your fatigue and stress

- Use your positive, happy and uplifting Affirmations Life Tools daily.
- During the day, take several short naps or breaks in a comfortable chair rather than in bed.
- Go for short walks or do some light exercise whenever you can.
- Try easier or shorter versions of your usual activities.
- Ask your family or friends to help you with tasks that you find difficult or tiring.
- Re-assess your priorities and save your energy for the things that are most important to you.

Talk to an oncology social worker or nurse about your negative side effects. These professionals can also help you manage fatigue, stress and worry. They can work with you to deal with any emotional or practical concerns that may be causing discomfort and symptoms and help you develop ways to cope.

Use your own voice recording

Listen to the audio recording that you created with your own voice and wake up trusting that your strength and vitality are returning, enabling you to feel excited about living your life.

Message from your affirmation life coach

You are using your wondrous inner power to create miracles in your life. You are breathing fresh, new life into your body. I am so proud of you and your wonderful work. Keep it up!

Affirmations when properly done always work!
(although not always within our preferred time frame or the way we think they should work)

FEAR

Fear short-circuits the cosmic energy that flows throughout your body, inhibiting your cells and creating toxins that can be injurious to your organs, tissues and every part of your body. Any negative thought, if fertilized, can develop into a real fear monster that can tear you down. That's why it's so important to learn how to handle fear before it creates stress in your body. As fear can be a major concern when undergoing chemo or other medical treatments, I have included a few extra tools to help you cope. For me, these tools were entertaining, and particularly powerful in addressing my fears.

My experience with fear

With most of the negative side effects that I experienced, there was a lot of fear. My immediate fear was that the side effects would be permanent and that I would have to deal with them for the rest of my life. This led to the fear of being disabled and needing to have other people take care for me, which led to other fears. I found that if I did not immediately deal with it, the fear would quickly permeate every part of my body and result in panic. So, before that happened, I used the following fear-releasing tools and found that they really helped me. They didn't completely take away that fear, but they did calm me down so I could think more clearly and take better care of myself.

Mentally Accept the Worst exercise

I accepted the fact that I was a cancer patient and taking chemotherapy. Then I immediately started to think of ways that I could mitigate the negative effects or help myself deal with them. This gave my mind something tangible and positive to think about and focus upon. Remember: Affirmation Life Tools do not necessarily take the negative side effects away (although they often do); however, they really *do* help you cope and manage them better.

Clap it Clear exercise

Some people have a real fear of the dark, especially when doing chemotherapy or radiation. In the same way that certain lamps can be turned on and off by clapping, you can clap your hands when a fear appears, and imagine it immediately dissipating. Affirm out loud: "Light is everywhere. There is nothing to be afraid of. The light is here to guide me!" This immediately changes your mood and helps you deal with and/or release your fear of the dark. Then say: "I am safe and secure!"

Stop Sign exercise

I use my Stop Sign exercise in many situations. When a negative side effect pops up with its companion fear, I pick up one of my Stop Signs, look at it and then say very loudly, "Stop!" At the same time, I snap the elastic band that I keep on my wrist, or stamp my foot. Then I visualize my fear going, going, gone! This stops my fear in its tracks and brings my focus back into the present moment.

Find Enlightening Answers Readily exercise

My acronym for fear is:
Find
Enlightening
Answers
Readily

This tool encourages you to think things through and focus on finding positive solutions. Find out why you are afraid and then *find enlightening answers readily* to help you mitigate or release whatever is bothering you. Every time the fear kicks in, clear your mind and ask yourself what you're afraid of. Accept the answer and then direct your mind towards coming up with creative solutions for dealing with it. You are in charge of your mind and you can direct it wherever you choose. Let your fear become a reminder to immediately switch your focus towards finding enlightening answers readily, using the power of your mind and your faith in your own ability to heal.

Deflecting Negativity affirmation

If you encounter negative people who project their own fears onto you, regarding cancer, use it as an opportunity to declare your positive affirmations out loud, and to validate yourself for taking charge of your own healing.

For example, if someone says to you, "Oh, that's awful. You must be really scared. How do you cope?" Say: "I'm managing very well, thank you. I'm getting stronger and healthier every day and I'm taking really good care of my body. I'm committed to being completely healed and well!"

Prayer and believing

I respect every person's belief system. Prayer and believing are high on the Affirmation Life Tool list for everything. Go within and find what it is that you believe in, whether it's God, the universal life force, nature or the power of your amazing body, and then use it to nourish yourself spiritually. Faith is a very important part of the affirmation program and it has helped numerous people worldwide to overcome their physical challenges. Set aside certain times of your day to focus, pray and give thanks for the blessings you have received and are about to receive. Some people find that joining with me in my Nightly World Affirmation/Prayer is very comforting and helpful. Details can be found on my website: www.annemariesangelchapel.com.

Give It All You've Got exercise

One of my young friends shared with me her approach to dealing with intense fear. She said that a sudden panic attack descended on her while driving. She pulled over in a safe place, stopped the car, rolled up the windows, locked the doors and said to her fear: "Okay, Mr Fear, give me everything you've got! Sock it to me—all of it! Come on, do it!" She was amazed that after doing this exercise her intense fear lifted, as if by magic, and she began to relax. She proved to herself that when you name your fear, face it, and talk to it directly, it loses its power over you. I acknowledge her for having the courage to face her fear head-on and not let it run her.

Cancel, Cancel affirmation

When that nasty old fear comes up, be ready for it. As soon as you start feeling scared or vulnerable, prone to negative or catastrophic thinking, say to yourself: "Cancel, cancel those negative thoughts/statements!" and then immediately fill that space with a positive thoughts or words, such as: "I am now safe and secure."

Fear Dragon exercise

Imagine your fear taking shape in front of you, in the form of a dragon. How big is it? What colour is it? What shape is it? How close is it? Can you feel its breath? How hot is it? Do you feel uncomfortable?

In your mind's eye, imagine picking up a club and pushing the dragon away from you. You are stronger than any dragon. Ask it to speak to you. Say: "Have you anything to say to me?" Listen with your inner ear. You may be very interested at what it says to you. Be firm with it and inform it that it has no place in your body or around you and that it has to go, now!

Should the dragon try to hang around, say again: "You must go now! You are not welcome in or around me. You have no power over me. I am the powerful force here and you must obey me. I am the boss." Be firm and the dragon will vanish completely. Now, in the empty space that you have just created, imagine a colourful image that represents how you wish to feel or what you want to accomplish. This exercise is very effective in banishing any limiting fears and directing your heart and mind towards positive outcomes.

Fear Zoo exercise

This is another creative exercise that you can have fun with, and it can help you to put your fear into proper perspective. Imagine forming your own 'Fear Zoo'—a place where you can put all the animals that represent your fears. What animals would you choose? You might fear a wild tiger in the jungle, but would you fear a tiger in a zoo? I visualized my own 'Fear Zoo' as a contained, safe space where I can house all my fears—and even chat with them.

- I visualize my fear of seeing a doctor as a tiger.
- I imagine my fear of needles, treatments and having my blood pressure taken as a monkey.
- I imagine my fear of a negative side effect becoming permanent as a grizzly bear.

I visit them, in my mind, as often as possible. I look forward to our conversations and discussions. I consider them to be valuable teachers and I learn from my interactions with them. The tiger explained to me how important it was for me to visit my doctor regularly, to keep everything working in good order. He mentioned how grateful I should be that I have access to medical treatments. The monkey laughed at me and said, "You've been through a lot in your life. Are you really going to allow a tiny needle and getting your blood pressure taken to worry you?" The grizzly bear was surprisingly kind, gentle and wise. He looked at me and said, "First of all, tell that fear that it has to go. Don't waste that valuable brain power. Focus instead on using what you know about affirmations to help you through these side effects and then share that information with others in similar situations." Wow! They had all the answers. I was grateful for the supportive company they provided for me, and for their suggestions and advice.

At times, in my mind, I just sit quietly among them, feeling their presence. When you give fear a name and form and speak directly to it, its hold over you is lessened and it can even become your friend, offering unexpected wisdom and insights. What is your greatest fear? Name it, give it a form and speak directly to it, in the safety and control of your own powerful mind.

Your fear becomes manageable when you do this exercise. As long as you continue to grow and learn, you will have fears. Isn't it better to manage fear than to let it control you? Tell that fear that it has to go, and take charge of you with these tools. The mind does not differentiate between the real and the unreal.

Holly, one of my readers, shared her experience with the Fear Zoo exercise:

Fear was my constant companion. It followed me everywhere. I did the Fear Zoo exercise you teach in your book and am now coping one day at a time. No, not all of the fear has left me, but I am now able to leave my house and do the shopping (something I could never do). I am doing my affirmations daily and I KNOW I am becoming more and more free of fear. You are the greatest anti-fear teacher ever!

Discussing your fears

Once you know your fears, you can tell your doctor or nurse exactly what you are afraid of—whether it's needles or having an IV put in, being in a hospital or clinic, or the way you'll feel while getting chemotherapy. If you can tell your healthcare team what makes you nervous, they can usually figure out a way to help you. For example, if you're afraid of getting an IV put in your hand or arm, your doctor can make sure you have a sedative or a local anesthetic to numb the area. The key to the best treatment is good communication between you and your doctor. This is especially true with regard to managing any fears of undergoing chemotherapy/radiation or other medical treatments. Talking to your healthcare team or a support group can empower you and help you take actions that will reduce your fear.

Use your own voice recording

Listen to the audio recording that you created with your own voice and wake up trusting that all fear has disappeared from your body and you are at peace.

Message from your affirmation life coach

You are leaving your fear behind and are enjoying life in a much more relaxed and peaceful state. Wow. What can I say? In the game of life, you're a winner! You're amazing!

Affirmations when properly done always work!
(although not always within our preferred time frame or the way we think they should work)

GENERAL CIRCULATION (IMPAIRED)

Borrow Back exercise

Go back in your mind to a time when you had perfect, healthy circulation in your entire body. Remember feeling energized, happy and full of vitality, with everything flowing easily through all of your cells and body systems.

I was amazed at how tapping into an earlier memory actually created abundant healthy circulation in my body! This is a very powerful technique and you cannot overuse it. There is always more where that came from. I suggest you use this exercise for any positive feeling that you wish to re-create in your body. Whenever you begin to feel that your body is not working perfectly, go back to some earlier positive memory (image) and transport it into your present moment. And don't forget to say thank you for all your blessings.

1% Solution affirmation

"Today, my circulation is 1% better than it was yesterday." Say this every day until you reach your desired goal. Or you could say: "Today, I am feeling wonderful energy coursing through my body. I know that in 30 days I will be 30% better." If an improvement of 10% per day seems feasible to you, then use that percentage. Just be sure that whatever you're affirming feels within the realm of possibility, so your mind will not object and cancel it out.

Note: You may wish to do some exercises for increasing your general circulation. Create a program specially tailored for you, taking into consideration your age, health condition and lifestyle. Make it a routine and be consistent!

Use your own voice recording

Listen to the audio recording you created with your voice and wake up trusting that you now have increased healthy circulation throughout your entire body.

Message from your affirmation life coach

The Affirmation Life Tools are certainly working for you. Keep up the good work! And keep affirming how happy you are to have great, healthy circulation in every part of your body.

Affirmations when properly done always work!
(although not always within our preferred time frame or the way we think they should work)

HAIR LOSS

Affirming and Anchoring Hair affirmation

Find a comfortable place to sit where you will not be disturbed. Relax, take some deep breaths and tell yourself that this is your special creative time for you. Rub your head gently, saying: "My hair is becoming healthier and healthier. It is now becoming thick and beautiful. I love you, I bless you and I thank you for making my hair healthy." Take time to feel the increased circulation on your scalp and in your head. As you rub your head gently, you are anchoring your words (affirmations). When I used this affirmation, I added the following words, which really worked for me: "Grow, little hairs, grow!"

Borrow Back exercise

Remember a time when your hair was very healthy, thick and beautiful, and transport this image into the present moment. Then imagine already having that thick, healthy, beautiful hair back again, right now. It is exactly as you wish it to be and you see it in your mind's eye every single day, every time you look in the mirror. Love, respect and approve of your hair. Say over and over: "I love my beautiful, thick, healthy hair." Stimulate your scalp daily by briskly rubbing it to get the circulation flowing.

Stop Sign exercise

Remember the stop sign you learned about earlier? It's time to use it again. Pick it up, look at it and say, very loudly: "Stop!" to the hair loss. Say to your hair: "You must stop falling out and start growing new hair now!" When you say this, either stamp your foot or make some other physical movement to strengthen the command. Know that this works as you have re-directed your thoughts!

This Too Shall Pass affirmation

Focus your attention on your head and hair. Thank it for serving you so well for all these years and giving you beautiful, thick, healthy hair. Say: "I love you, I bless you and I thank you for giving me beautiful hair for many years. I know that this hair loss is not coming from you or from my body; it is one of the side effects of chemotherapy and it is temporary. This too shall pass!"

Healthy Hair affirmation

Use the following affirmation to focus your mind on restoring your healthy hair, or make up your own.

Master affirmation for beautiful, healthy hair

I, [your name], deserve and now have thick, healthy, beautiful hair. My hair is growing stronger each day. I take care of my hair using the right shampoo and conditioner for my hair and giving my head frequent massages. Each strand of hair is becoming healthy, shiny and beautiful. People remark on the great condition of my hair. I am happy and fulfilled, to the good of all parties concerned. Thank you, thank you, thank you.

I fully accept.

Signed _____ *Dated* _____

Managing hair loss

Not all anti-cancer medicines cause hair loss; your doctor or nurse can tell you whether you might be affected. Hair loss is often one of the more frustrating aspects of cancer treatment. When hair falls out, it can affect self-image and quality of life, but there are ways to cope with this temporary side effect.

Today, there are lovely wigs that are made to look and feel like human hair. You may wish to purchase one to get you through this uncomfortable phase. Some wigs are made so well and look so real that people cannot tell the difference between the wig and your own hair. Some patients cover their heads when going out in public and still others go out as they are. Do what feels right for you.

Everyone's experience is different, so it is important to talk with your doctor or nurse about how your particular treatment affects hair loss. Depending on the treatment, hair loss may start anywhere from 7 to 21 days after the first chemotherapy session. Hair starts to grow back when you have finished the treatment. It may have a different texture or colour, but these changes are usually not permanent. My chemo doctor told me that I would not lose all my hair and I did not, but my hair seemed to be a lot thinner and lifeless. I did lose some of my hair during the chemo treatment, but I did what I could to keep as much hair as possible.

Dyeing eyebrows and/or hair

I was advised to refrain from having my eyebrows dyed until six months after finishing my chemo treatments. I am a natural blonde so I did not have to worry about hair dyeing, but I think the same advice would hold true for dyeing one's hair while taking treatments or shortly after.

What I did for my hair during my chemo treatment

I am so blessed to have a dear friend, Heike Bogner, as my hairdresser. She set up a schedule to help stop my hair from falling out and to help make my hair healthier. She used special all-natural hair-care products designed to add volume and vitality to hair that has become limp and lifeless, due to chemo, shock, stress, hormonal issues and other factors.

You can use these before, during and after chemo to help keep your hair looking healthy. Certain salons carry these products, or you can purchase them online. When Heike started working with my hair during my chemo, it was lifeless, dull, dry and limp. Over the weekly treatments, however, she noticed new hair growth and a steady improvement in the overall health of my hair. It actually felt stronger. Now that I have finished the chemo treatments, there is great hair growth and my hair is returning to its natural shiny, healthy state.

Use your own voice recording

Listen to the audio recording that you created with your own voice and wake up feeling uplifted, trusting that you already have increased hair growth and healthy circulation in your head and whole body.

Message from your affirmation life coach

Congratulations on your dedication and perseverance in using your Affirmation Life Tools. Your work is really paying off as you are already starting to see the good results. Keep going!

Affirmations when properly done always work!
(although not always within our preferred time frame or the way we think they should work)

HEADACHE

Whiteboard exercise

Visualize a whiteboard with a marker in front of you. Take the marker and write, 'Headache.' Then erase that word and write, "Headache going, going, gone!" Imagine the headache being given notice that it is not welcome in your healthy body. Take a deep breath, breathing out any pain or discomfort. Then take another deep breath, breathing in healing, peace and joy. Stay with this feeling of complete comfort and happiness for a few minutes, saying to yourself, "Thank you, thank you, thank you," knowing that your body's excellent healing mechanism is working ideally for you.

Abbreviation affirmation

You can use an abbreviated version of any affirmation, in the following way. At the top of a page, write your affirmation—for example: "My chemo/medical treatment is working harmoniously." Then write down the first letter of each word (in this case, mcmtiwh) a total of 77 times, while repeating the affirmation out loud.

1% Solution affirmation

Terry, one of my readers, shared the following story with me, and I used her approach in creating the 1% Solution affirmation.

> When lying in a hospital bed in excruciating pain, with one tube sticking out of my nose and another one out of my belly, I found it very difficult, if not downright impossible, to say, "I am 100% healthy." So I devised a way to have it work for me. I said, "Today, I am 1% better than I was yesterday!" That worked for me because my mind could and did believe that I was 1% better and made it happen.

One of the participants in my chemo class told me that he suffered from a severe and continuous headache for at least two months after radiation treatments. He used this affirmation and was very grateful for the information.

When you are experiencing a headache that just won't go away, do the following 1% Solution affirmation:

Say to your body, "Today, my headache is 1% less than it was yesterday. All pain and discomfort in my head area is now leaving." Repeat this affirmation daily with faith, passion, belief and expectancy over and over. Should your faith be strong enough to really believe you can be 10% better in one day, then use that percentage.

When I did this process, I started off using the 1% and was so delighted with the results that I soon increased the percentage. Whatever percentage you choose, it needs to be believable for you and, when it is, your powerful mind immediately begins to create the appropriate conditions in the body for your optimum health.

Jack, a chemo patient, also shared his story with me. He said one day he felt the beginnings of a migraine headache. He remembered what I had shared in a workshop about talking to your body and how powerful our mind is, so he said, with authority and faith: "Stop! There is no need for you here. You must leave now!" And it did! Jack demonstrated the power of the subconscious mind, which obeys the conscious mind when given clear, strong instructions. How are you instructing your subconscious mind?

Heather, one of my readers, says: "Just saying these words—*I am now becoming healthier and healthier and headache-free*—actually helped alleviate my headache. Now, I'm visualizing myself as happy, healthy and completely pain-free."

Use your own voice recording

Listen to the audio recording that you created with your own voice and wake up feeling happy and grateful that your headaches will no longer be an issue.

Message from your affirmation life coach

Feel how clear, calm and pain-free your head is becoming. You are weathering the storms of life with faith and persistence and will soon be reaping the wonderful benefits! Enjoy!

Affirmations when properly done always work!
(although not always within our preferred time frame or the way we think they should work)

HEART ISSUES

Talk to your body

Visualize your heart being strong and healthy, pumping perfectly and steadily, for your highest good. Relax, meditate and do your best to be calm, so your heart can work positively for you. Act as if your heart is already strong and healthy, saying often during the day, "Strong, healthy heart, me, now!" Thank your heart for its unfailing performance for you, from the moment you were born.

1% Solution affirmation

If you feel that your heart is not working as smoothly or healthily as you would wish, use the 1% Solution affirmation. Say: "Today, my heart is 1% healthier, better, calmer than it was yesterday." Repeat this statement daily with as much faith, passion, belief and expectancy as possible (and remember to make sure that whatever you are affirming is believable for you).

Toothbrush Forgiveness affirmation

Tell your body that you are sorry for not taking better care of it—especially your heart. Be grateful for all the wonderful work your heart has done and continues to do for you, every single day. Then do the Toothbrush Forgiveness affirmation. When you brush your teeth in the morning, look at yourself in the mirror and say: "Hey, self, you are a wonderful person. I now forgive everyone and everything that has ever hurt me. I now forgive myself for not eating properly, exercising, releasing excess stress and for not taking better care of my heart. I love, respect and approve of myself just the way I am." Keep affirming these thoughts in your mind as you brush, and imagine all regrets and resentments flowing down the drain as you rinse your teeth.

Florence, one of my readers, shared the following story with me:

> Many, many thanks for your support and healing affirmations throughout Tim's horrendous heart surgery. He is recovering well with no heart problems and no breathing problems. He is able to come up the back stairs without stopping or puffing. We kept on affirming that his surgery would go well and that he would heal quickly and completely, and it is fast becoming a reality. Am I hooked on the power of properly done affirming and the spoken word? You bet! We both are!

Use your own voice recording

Listen to the audio recording that you created with your own voice and wake up trusting that your heart is strong, healthy and functioning perfectly.

Message from your affirmation life coach

I am so impressed with your great progress. Your heart is becoming healthier and stronger every day. You are creating healthy conditions in your entire body by your positive affirming and visualizing. You inspire me!

Affirmations when properly done always work!
(although not always within our preferred time frame or the way we think they should work)

IMMUNE SYSTEM (COMPROMISED)

Spiritual Disinfectant exercise

Get a small spray bottle, fill it with water, and add a drop or two of your favourite essential oil. (Or you might wish to try some oregano oil, which has strong antiviral and antibiotic properties.) On masking tape, write with a felt-tip pen the following words: Spiritual Disinfectant, and place the tape on the spray bottle. Whenever you find yourself in an uncomfortable situation or among others who are ill, spray some of your Spiritual Disinfectant around you. If that's not practical, visualize doing it, knowing that your mind does not differentiate between the real and the imagined. This is a powerful way to dispel negative energy and cleanse the air around you.

Note: Never spray anyone in the face. Spray around your face and body and anywhere you feel needs it.

Connie, one of my readers, uses a spiritual disinfectant spray with her students. She calls it her 'Special Spray', which is a blend of essential oil and water. "Whenever any of the children in my class say something negative to themselves or one another, my 'Special Spray' comes out to eat up the negative words," she says. "I spray it over their heads (they have their eyes closed) and when they open their eyes they usually have a smile on their faces. Thank you!"

Shower exercise

Take a shower and, as you rub soap on your body, visualize it cleansing every speck of negativity and fear from your system. See the cleansing water going down the drain, taking with it all germs and infection from your body, and making your body squeaky-clean. Now allow clean warm water to pour over you, from the top of your head to the tips of your toes. Feel the healing energy giving strength and vitality to your immune system and your entire body. Step out of the shower and dry yourself off as vigorously as possible, to stimulate healthy circulation. Then get dressed and get on with your day, giving thanks for the wonderful gift of health from your body.

Picture Power exercise

From the Internet, print off a diagram of your immune system, with all the various organs, lymph nodes and blood cells involved. Look at the picture and focus your attention on all the parts of your body that are being healed of any disease or condition, and visualize healing power flowing into every cell. Imagine your immune system becoming healthier and having abundant energy to fight off germs and anything that is not for your body's highest good.

Protect your body

You may wish to add a couple of drops of oregano oil to a glass of water and drink it. This oil is very potent, so you might wish to start with one drop, to see how your body tolerates it. When visiting hospitals or any large gatherings, it can be a good idea to use your Spiritual Disinfectant spray before you go out. Spray all around you, asking for complete protection from any harmful germs or negativity. I also add a couple of drops of oregano oil to the water when I'm washing my hands.

Good practice

I would also suggest visualizing a protective dome of white light around your body, from the roots of your hair to the tips of your toes, every day and every night. When driving, I always visualize a dome of white light over me, my vehicle, any passengers and everyone around me before starting my car.

Use your own voice recording

Listen to the audio recording that you created with your own voice and wake up trusting and feeling grateful that your immune system has been fortified and revitalized.

Message from your affirmation life coach

Feel your immune system being strengthened daily. You are weaving a beautiful tapestry of unconditional love and health by caring for yourself so completely. I am proud of you.

Affirmations when properly done always work!
(although not always within our preferred time frame or the way we think they should work)

METALLIC TASTE IN MOUTH

Mentally Accept the Worst exercise

Take a few moments to mentally accept the worst that could possibly happen, given that this metallic taste might prevent you from eating properly, to heal yourself. Then, immediately find ways to mitigate or handle it. This gives your mind a few moments to gather some constructive thoughts so you don't panic. If you experience a metallic taste in your mouth (as many do, with chemo), accept the fact that it is a side effect of the chemotherapy treatment and is temporary. Keep affirming that this too shall pass, and it usually does.

Going, Going, Gone affirmation

When I had that unpleasant metallic taste in my mouth, I worried that it would be permanent and affect the taste of my food. I visualized writing the following words on a whiteboard with a marker: *The metallic taste in my mouth.* Then I imagined writing over those words, *Going, going, gone!* I looked at these words for a few seconds, took a deep breath and then erased everything I had just written, saying, "The metallic taste in my mouth is now gone!"

Repeating this simple 'Going, Going, Gone' affirmation over and over really helped me to ease this condition and it is slowly leaving my body.

Stop Sign exercise

You can always use your stop sign whenever any side effect bothers you. I pick it up, look at it and then say very loudly, "Stop!" and I stamp my foot to anchor that command. I say, "This metallic taste is not welcome in my mouth or body. You must go, now!" I am very firm and my fear quickly dissipates. I believe this affirmation works because our mind is given a very clear command, which it will obey if we are forceful with our words and thoughts.

Use your own voice recording

Listen to the audio recording that you created with your own voice and wake up trusting that the metallic taste is now leaving, never to return!

Message from your affirmation life coach

Just as the sun comes up every day and shines upon you, your taste buds are being restored to their normal, healthy state. Congratulations are in order.

Affirmations when properly done always work!
(although not always within our preferred time frame or the way we think they should work)

MOUTH SORES

I found mouth sores to be very painful and irritating, and I made good use of my Affirmation Life Tools to help me cope with and finally get rid of them.

Flashlight exercise

On a sheet of white paper, I wrote in huge letters, 'CLEAR OF MOUTH SORES, ME, NOW!' I put the paper and the flashlight in my bathroom, where it was dark at night. If I got up in the middle of the night to use the bathroom, I aimed my flashlight at those words on the paper and switched it on and off three times. I repeated this process three times and then went back to bed and immediately fell asleep again. Flashing the images into your brain by turning off and on of the light reinforces the message that you want your brain to see and remember. It's a powerful tool that works well for many.

Oil of oregano

Put a couple of drops of oregano oil in a glass of water and rinse your mouth thoroughly. Visualize and feel your mouth becoming vibrantly healthy, and imagine this wonderful healing oil removing every speck of negative material and healing every mouth sore as you gently swill it around your mouth. Spit out the mixture and then take a couple more drops of the oil in a glass of water and drink it, directing it to clear up any infection in your body.

You may wish to start with one drop in water, as the oil is very strong. Increase to two or three drops the next time, if you tolerate it well. This is my constant companion and is said to be one of nature's most powerful disinfectants. I have heard of flight attendants swallowing a few drops of oil of oregano in water to ward off germs before going on flights.

Use your own voice recording

Listen to the audio recording that you created with your own voice and wake up feeling grateful that your mouth is now becoming totally healthy.

Message from your affirmation life coach

You are on the right track and I am impressed with your progress. Say thank you to your wonderful self for your healed mouth, and enjoy your day.

Affirmations when properly done always work!
(although not always within our preferred time frame or the way we think they should work)

NAILS (SPLITTING, WEAK)

During chemotherapy, patients sometimes experience changes to their fingernails and toenails. I noticed that my nails were splitting, weak and discoloured. When I finished the chemo treatment, however, they started coming back to their normal state, slowly but surely. I found some gentle nail strengtheners and used them regularly. A nail strengthener is a special type of nail polish that can strengthen the nails when applied regularly. I used dark-coloured nail polish to protect the nails from sunlight and I found that black, dark brown or navy polish worked best for me.

Photograph exercise

Find a picture of your own nails when they were healthy and beautiful. If you don't have one, use a picture of someone else's healthy nails, from a magazine or from the Internet. Look at this picture and mentally absorb it. Then engage your five physical senses:

See how beautiful your nails are becoming.

Hear people commenting on your healthy nails.

Feel how happy you are with them looking so healthy.

Smell your favourite flower or essential oil.

Taste some fresh, sparkling water or visualize biting into a juicy apple.

Act as if

Act as if your nails are already healthy and in perfect condition. Muster up as much happy, positive feeling as you possibly can and get excited about it! The more positive feeling you can generate, the more effectively your body and mind will work to bring your nails into alignment with that feeling.

Some tips
- Keep your nails clipped short.
- Regularly apply moisturizing cream to your nails and cuticles.
- Wash your hands often to prevent infection.
- Wear protective gloves when doing housework.

Use your own voice recording

Listen to the audio recording that you created with your own voice and wake up feeling grateful for your beautiful, healthy nails.

Message from your affirmation life coach

I'm very proud of you. You're becoming aware of and using your wondrous inner power by regularly using these Affirmation Life Tools. I believe in you and the powerful choices you are making and affirming for yourself. Great stuff!

Affirmations when properly done always work!
(although not always within our preferred time frame or the way we think they should work)

NAUSEA

Nausea is one of the most common side effects of chemotherapy, and it is often one of the most difficult to deal with. The following affirmations and exercises will help to ease your nausea, to keep you positive and to remind you that this side effect will soon be gone.

Bless your food before eating

I blessed my food before I ate and I made a sincere effort to eat and drink slowly. I ate small meals and avoided sweets and fried or fatty foods. I made sure that I always had my prescribed anti-nausea medication handy at home. I had plenty of water and/or other fluids to drink and I followed the hospital dietician's advice as much as possible.

Love your Chemo affirmation

When you feel nauseous taking chemo pills or treatment, you're in a relationship with them so do your best to make that relationship healthy, sound and fulfilling. See your chemo treatment as your friend. Trust that it's helping to make and keep you cancer-free.

Hold the pills in your hand and say: "I send you love, I bless you and I thank you for working harmoniously with every part of my body, for my highest good." When taking other treatments, such as intravenous drips or radiation, say: "Chemo/radiation treatment, I send you love, I bless you and I thank you for clearing out all the negative and unhealthy debris and making my body strong and healthy, starting right now."

1% Solution affirmation

If you feel unable to believe that your stomach and intestinal area could be 100% healthy, do the 1% Solution affirmation. Say: "Today, my stomach and intestines are 1% better than they were yesterday." Repeat this statement daily, with as much faith, passion, belief and expectancy as you possibly can. If you're feeling more positive and optimistic, affirm that you are now 10% calmer or better. Just be sure that whatever you are affirming is believable for you! You can repeat this statement over and over as many times as you wish.

Flushing out Nausea exercise

I visualized every speck of nausea being dumped into a container and flushed down the toilet. As I imagined watching it slowly going down the drain, I took a deep, slow breath, visualizing all fear, pain, sick feelings and negativity in my body evaporating right before my eyes. Then I quickly filled the space that I had just created with pure health, joy and happiness. I found this exercise to be especially powerful and I had tears sliding down my cheeks as I whispered, "Thank you, thank you, thank you."

Any time a sick thought or feeling tried to attach itself to me, I said my 'Cancel, cancel' affirmation to immediately cancel that negative thought, quickly replacing it with: "I am healthy, happy, calm and at peace."

Coping with nausea and vomiting

My doctor gave me a prescription for nausea, which really helped me. I noticed a big difference when I took the pills as directed.

Anti-vomiting affirmation

I used the following affirmation to help calm my stomach whenever I felt nauseous. "My stomach and intestines are at peace. I am calm and in control of my body. When I need to release some negative substance from my body, I do so easily and quickly. I am a powerful health magnet."

Recently, I had Dr Bernie Siegel as a guest on the Dr Anne Marie Evers Talk Show and he shared the following story. A woman who was undergoing chemotherapy vomited every time after her treatment. Her husband purchased some bags and had them in the car, ready for her to use when she came out. One day, when she got in the car after her treatment, he handed her a bag. The woman opened the bag and found a dozen roses inside. She never vomited again. Isn't it interesting how our minds work?

Use your own voice recording

Listen to the audio recording that you created with your own voice and wake up feeling grateful that your stomach and intestines are calm and peaceful.

Message from your affirmation life coach

Now that you have taken the appropriate action, watch your affirmations manifest right before your eyes. Feel your stomach and intestines becoming calmer and more relaxed. I am proud of you and your creative healing work!

Affirmations when properly done always work!
(although not always within our preferred time frame or the way we think they should work)

NERVE AND CELL DAMAGE

Understanding magnetism

The Magic Magnetic Health Circle that I refer to in this book is your personal aura—the energy field that extends outwards for several feet around your body. Everyone's aura is unique, just as every fingerprint is unique, and it is in constant communication with our external world, transmitting and receiving energy and messages, and acting as a magnet for certain situations, people and challenges in our lives. Magnetism is the mysterious cosmic power that holds the earth, sun, moon, stars and the whole solar system in space. Through positive thinking, feeling and action, we can become magnets for positive outcomes and dynamics, attracting similar thoughts, people and situations to us. Some scientists believe this magnetism is created in our body's cells, which can be programmed negatively or positively, depending on our outlook and beliefs. If there are no conflicting, negative thoughts to hinder or negate our positive thoughts, and if the thoughts are concentrated and focused on an image, they have the power to produce the positive outcomes we have affirmed.

With focused intention, action and healthy self-care, we can boost the size and health of our energy field, thereby often boosting our energy levels and vitality. The following exercise is designed to make you more aware of your aura, while visualizing it as a field of healing energy that can help you get well.

Magic Magnetic Health Circle affirmation

Stand in front of a window and, with your arms outstretched from your sides, slowly turn clockwise, saying these words: "I, [*your name*], now magnetize into my Magic Magnetic Health Circle [your aura], from the creator, sun, moon, stars and entire solar system, complete healing for all the nerves and cells in my body. I am becoming calm, relaxed and peaceful." Complete the exercise by saying: "Thank you, thank you, thank you." Do this procedure slowly, three times, allowing each word to sink deep into your subconscious mind so that it can manifest as affirmed.

Managing nerve damage

It is important to tell your doctor as soon as possible if you experience serious side effects. He/she may want to adjust some of your medications or chemotherapy. They may also want to see if there is another reason for the problem that can be treated. (When my husband suddenly passed away, while I was undergoing chemo, my doctor adjusted my treatments as I was in a state of shock and grief.) Nerve damage is usually temporary, but it can take time for the nerves to heal. In the meantime, and as I mentioned previously, take extra caution when handling hot, sharp or dangerous objects. Use handrails on stairs and in the tub or shower.

While on chemotherapy, I experienced some numbness and tingling in my hands and feet—what doctors call peripheral neuropathy. Symptoms related to neuropathy and other types of nerve damage can include the following:

- Difficulty picking up objects or buttoning clothing
- Problems with balance
- Difficulty walking
- Hearing loss
- Dropping things
- Inability to open jars, cans etc, due to reduced strength or flexibility.

Use your own voice recording

Listen to the audio recording that you created with your own voice and wake up feeling grateful for the complete repair of all nerves and cells damaged by the chemotherapy treatment.

Message from your affirmation life coach

Congratulations on using the Magic Magnetic Health Circle affirmation for this particular side effect. It is working for you. Don't give up now. Keep going!

Affirmations when properly done always work!
(although not always within our preferred time frame or the way we think they should work)

NIGHTMARES

I experienced some very disturbing nightmares when I was undergoing chemo treatments, so I made sure that I didn't watch any scary or negative movies/TV shows before going to bed. I always filled my mind with happy and positive thoughts. I also played my own voice recording every night, affirming vibrant health for my whole body.

Before you go to sleep, prepare yourself by saying that you will have a wonderful, peaceful, restful sleep and will wake up refreshed and excited to greet the new day. If a nightmare wakes you up, sit up or get up and visualize a happy, positive picture of you being safe, protected and happy.

White Light exercise

At bedtime, visualize a beautiful white light all around you—a dome of protection that extends from the top of your head to the tips of your toes and stays in place all night. You are protected and safe, and can sleep in peace.

Clap it Clear exercise

To help you with this visualization, you might wish to purchase a lamp that turns on and off when you clap your hands. Then, when you have a nightmare, clap your hands to turn on the light, saying to yourself: "I am safe, secure and peaceful. There is nothing to be afraid of." Then clap your hands again to turn the light off, and imagine the nightmare going with it. Go back to enjoying a sound and restful sleep and wake up refreshed. If you can't find a lamp that turns on/off in this way, visualize it in your mind as vividly as you can.

Use your own voice recording

Listen to the audio recording that you created with your own voice and allow it to take you into a peaceful sleep so that you wake up feeling rested and happy.

Message from your affirmation life coach

Only you can master your mind, as you are doing, with these powerful visualizations and affirmations for evaporating your fears and nightmares. I am confident in your abilities. Enjoy your restful sleep and increased energy.

Affirmations when properly done always work!
(although not always within our preferred time frame or the way we think they should work)

NOSE (RUNNY)

I found this side effect very annoying. Shortly after I started chemo treatment, I found I needed to take a box of Kleenex with me everywhere I went. As I started using my Affirmation Life Tools, however, the dripping from my nose decreased and eventually stopped altogether.

Spiritual Disinfectant exercise

On a piece of masking tape, write 'Spiritual disinfectant' and put it on a small spray bottle. Fill the bottle with water and, if you wish, add a few drops of your favourite essential oil. If your nose starts dripping, simply spray the air around you, saying: "I now spray away this runny nose and all negative thoughts and situations. Thank you, thank you, thank you for my healed, healthy nose and whole body." I kept affirming that the runny nose was a temporary side effect of the chemo and that it would pass—and it did! Whenever that bothersome side effect came back, I said with great authority: "You must leave, now!" My nose is now functioning normally.

Going, Going, Gone affirmation

When I experienced a perpetually runny nose, I took a picture of my face (showing my nose clearly), then I wrote the following words below my nose: 'The condition of my nose constantly running is now going, going, gone!' Always be specific so that you don't create something you don't want. Be sure to say: "The situation of my nose dripping is now going, going, gone!" You certainly don't want to have your nose gone!

Use your own voice recording

Listen to the audio recording that you created with your own voice and wake up trusting that all unnecessary dripping from your nose has now stopped.

Message from your affirmation life coach

You are creating magic wherever you go, as you use these powerful tools to take charge of your body and mind. Don't forget to acknowledge and congratulate yourself on doing this challenging work.

Affirmations when properly done always work!
(although not always within our preferred time frame or the way we think they should work)

OVERWHELM

Hourglass exercise

If you do not already have one, purchase an hourglass. Place it on your desk or coffee table, in clear view. If you become overwhelmed, turn the hourglass upside down and notice how only one grain of sand goes through that narrow neck at a time. If you tried to force a lot more grains though that narrow space, they would get stuck. Take a lesson from this and know that you can only do ONE task properly at a time. If you try to do too many tasks at once, you are likely to get stuck in indecision, become stagnant and get nothing done. Bear in mind, too, that you can only really think one thought at a time!

Toothpick Pick-up exercise

When things are overwhelming for you, take a large handful of toothpicks and drop them so they scatter all over the floor. If you try to pick them all up at once, you'll find that it's impossible, but if you pick up one or a few at a time, you'll be able to complete the task. Doing this exercise can become like a meditation, stilling the mind as you focus on picking up each little toothpick. As you do this, reflect on how you could apply this process to your life. Doing what you can, mindfully and slowly, rather than trying to accomplish everything (including healing your body) at once, is a powerful way to focus the power of your mind for better results. Focus, concentrate and complete your work, activities and healing in manageable chunks, performing one task at a time.

Percentage Progress affirmation

This is one of my favourite tools and one that I used while writing this book. For example, I decided that this book would be 100 pages long; when I had written 25 pages, I said to myself: "Wow, I am a quarter of the way towards completing my book." Breaking the project down into fractions or percentages helped me to stay focused. It encouraged me to keep going and made it seem less overwhelming. Do this when you feel overwhelmed with things in your life, breaking them down into parts and acknowledging your progress every time you are 10%, 50% or 75% of the way there.

Thought-watching exercise

Are you overwhelmed, with too many negative thoughts running through your mind? It could be time to do some 'thought-watching' to find out exactly where your thoughts have taken up residency. If you're not happy with the outcome, in some area in your life, change your thoughts. You have that power, and only you can do it. After all, you took those thoughts in the first place, even if you originally absorbed them from someone else. For three days, keep track of your thoughts on a piece of paper or in a small notebook.

Make four columns with the following headings:

Same as yesterday	Negative	Positive	New

Do some thought-watching and put a checkmark under the appropriate column. When you add up the checkmarks in each column, you will be amazed at what you discover about yourself and your thinking.

Use your own voice recording

Listen to the audio recording that you created with your own voice and wake up trusting that you will complete all your tasks easily and effortlessly and in the allotted time frame.

Message from your affirmation life coach

Remember the hourglass and one grain of sand going through that tiny neck at a time? Be gentle with yourself and do just one task at a time. Notice how it focuses your mind and frees you up for enjoying many other things. You are a powerful creator.

Affirmations when properly done always work!
(although not always within our preferred time frame or the way we think they should work)

PAIN

I Am Handling It affirmation

Every time I experienced pain as a result of the chemotherapy, I had a huge helping of fear. Sometimes, I could feel the fear starting at the bottom of my feet and working its way up my body, becoming stronger and more intense, as it went. If I did not use my specific Affirmation Life Tools to stop or reduce that intense feeling, it quickly turned into panic. The fear that I experienced was that this negative side effect was permanent and I would have it for the rest of my life. At those times, I repeated the following words over and over: "I am handling it." Every time I did this, the pain and fear began to dissipate.

Talk to your body

Don't forget to communicate with your body and to allow it to communicate with you. Ask it the following questions: *What do you want me to know, by creating this pain? What lesson do I need to learn?* Sometimes, you will receive an answer quickly; at other times, it may make itself known to youa day or week later. Communicate daily with your body. The more you respect and heed its needs, the more powerfully and healthily it can serve you.

One Step at a Time affirmation

Don't forget to take one step at a time. When you are in pain, it's normal to want things to improve quickly, but try to be patient with your wonderful body, knowing that it is doing the very best it can. Every affirmation or exercise that you do contributes towards your healing, so it's important to trust in the process and to believe that your body can and will heal itself, with your conscious, diligent support.

For example, think of your pain disappearing in steps, as follows:

Step 1. You decide that your pain is not welcome in your body and you start releasing it.

Step 2. This is when you get serious and write out your master affirmation, saying: "I, [*your name*], deserve to be and now am free of pain. My body is becoming healthier and healthier. All pain in my body is leaving now!"

Step 3. Close your eyes and visualize these three words, in vivid colour: 'Going, going, gone'.

Say 'thank you' three times and live your day in an attitude of gratitude for being healthy and pain-free.

Pain-be-gone Spray affirmation

On a piece of masking tape, write the words: 'Pain-be-gone spray'. Place the tape on a small spray bottle. Fill the bottle with water and, if you wish, add a drop or two of your favourite essential oil. When you experience pain, say: "This pain affecting my body at this time is a side effect of chemo or medical treatments and not from my body and it is temporary. I now spray away all bodily aches, pains and discomfort."

Whenever you have pain, a negative thought or fear about your health, take out your disinfectant spray and use it! (You can also use the Stop Sign affirmation. Anita, a chemo patient, reports that using this affirmation stops her pain for several hours.)

Use your own voice recording

Listen to the audio recording that you created with your own voice and wake up trusting that all pain is leaving your body and you can relax!

Message from your affirmation life coach

Wow! Your wonderful affirmation work is rewarding you in so many ways. You are becoming healthier and healthier and free of all pain. Congratulations!

Affirmations when properly done always work!
(although not always within our preferred time frame or the way we think they should work)

RESTRICTED MOVEMENT

Are you experiencing difficulty moving your body? If so, use the following tools to help bring more ease and flexibility to your body and mind.

Mentally Accept the Worst exercise

Mentally accept the worst-case scenario regarding your restricted movement. Give yourself a few moments to consider this, then immediately start finding ways to mitigate, stop or handle it. This gives you time to gather your thoughts so you do not panic. Think of ways you could work with your body to improve your agility. Search out people and products that might help you. Take action so that your mind knows you're serious about taking charge and giving it a positive focus. Being proactive is always more powerful and effective than being passive and allowing your fears or illness to run your life. Once you start taking control of your mind, you'll find that things improve faster and more easily than you could have imagined.

Magic Magnetic Health Circle affirmation

Stand in front of the window and, with your arms outstretched from your sides, turn slowly in a clockwise direction, saying these words: "I, [*your name*], now magnetize into my Magic Magnetic Health Circle [aura], from the sun, moon, stars and entire solar system, free and easy movement of my entire body. Thank you, thank you, thank you."

Do this slowly three times, allowing each word to sink deep into your subconscious mind, where it can take root, grow and manifest as affirmed.

Use your own voice recording

Listen to the audio recording that you created with your own voice and wake up trusting that you now enjoy free movement, with no restrictions.

Message from your affirmation life coach

The Magic Magnetic Health Circle affirmation is working for you, bringing more freedom and movement of your body. Be proud of yourself for instructing your subconscious mind and trusting in a positive outcome.

Affirmations when properly done always work!
(although not always within our preferred time frame or the way we think they should work)

SELF-ESTEEM (LOW)

Sometimes, when people suffer a serious health challenge, they feel that they do not look their best. Maybe they are dropping too much weight and looking thin and gaunt or gaining too much and becoming overweight. They could be experiencing hair loss, dry, itchy skin and more. They may not be able to function normally in many aspects of life. When I became aware of feeling low self-esteem, unworthiness and other negative thoughts about myself, I created some powerful tools to get me back on track. The following two exercises worked particularly well for me.

Borrow Back exercise

When I was feeling exceptionally low in energy, with low self-esteem and self-worth, I mentally borrowed back a vivid, colourful picture of myself when I was full of vibrant energy, looking and feeling my very best. I chose a time when I felt complete, attractive and interesting; I was at an event where over a hundred people had gathered to hear me speak on the power of affirmations. I could feel the excitement welling up in me. I transported that wonderful image and feeling into the present moment, visualizing every detail.

I remembered exactly how my hair was done, my make-up, what I was wearing, and my jewellery. I transported that vivid colourful memory into my present moment. I felt as if it was really taking place. Then I felt a strong ray of hope, followed by excitement and expectancy, knowing that I could create this situation over and over in my life. Since the subconscious mind does not know the difference between the real and the unreal, between the seen and the unseen, I knew it would take action based on my words and help me to manifest a positive outcome.

Every time I felt uncomfortable, I willed myself to slip into the memory of that wonderful, happy, healthy time in my life and it worked miracles for me. When, in my mind, I put myself into that situation, it made me feel more peaceful, relaxed and hopeful. We should never underestimate the power of the mind over the body.

Block of Ice exercise

Visualize your body as a huge block of ice. Imagine chipping and chiselling away at it until you uncover the real healthy, confident and beautiful YOU hidden deep inside. Focus on forgiving and releasing all negativity, cutting away all that is not you. Visualize in vivid colour all cancer cells in your body being melted away, and a healthy, happy cancer-free image of you emerging from the block of ice. See your thick, healthy, beautiful hair; your clear, smooth, wrinkle-free and youthful skin; your body weighing your ideal weight; and being completely radiantly healthy in every way. Feel how confident and happy you are. Now your ice carving is complete and you are whole. See this image vividly in your mind and keep concentrating and focusing on it. Think it into existence. You have that creative power within you. Love, respect and approve of yourself, just the way you are. Then say thank you, thank you, thank you for the wonderful miracle of you!

Use your own voice recording

Listen to the audio recording that you created with your own voice and wake up knowing that your confidence, vitality and healthy self-esteem are already an integral part of you.

Message from your affirmation life coach

Wow! I am so proud of you and your wonderful success! When you are spreading your affirmation magic all around you, don't forget about the powerful positive impact you also have on others. You are unique and you are healing.

Affirmations when properly done always work!
(although not always within our preferred time frame or the way we think they should work)

SEX DRIVE (LOW)

You may experience a low sex drive as one of the side effects of chemotherapy. If so, use the following tools to help you cope with and improve the situation.

Magic Magnetic Health Circle affirmation

Stand in front of the window, slowly turn in a clockwise direction with your arms outstretched, saying the following master affirmation to yourself: "I, [*your name*], now magnetize into my Magic Magnetic Health Circle [my aura] health, peace, joy and happiness, which extends to everyone I meet. I am now cancer-free and radiantly healthy and I stay that way. I have a healthy sex drive and enjoy safe, healthy sex with my partner."

Borrow Back exercise

Relax your body and gently close your eyes. Mentally go back to a time when you were healthy and sexually active with your partner. See how sexy you looked, feel how great you felt, and hear your loved one telling you how much he/she loves you. Recall every single detail. Then mentally transport that vivid, colourful memory into the present moment, and keep that memory alive as you enjoy special loving moments with your partner.

To help you stay focused on regaining your full sexual health, repeat the following affirmation several times a day, while mentally recalling the positive, loving memory: "I, [*your name*], deserve and now enjoy having sex/making love with my partner. We exercise the desired control in our lovemaking and enjoy safe, fulfilling, healthy sex. We are considerate and loving with each other. We are happy, normal and balanced, to the good of all parties concerned."

Use your own voice recording

Listen to the audio recording that you created with your own voice and wake up trusting that you can now enjoy a healthy sex life with your partner.

Message from your affirmation life coach
A healthy, normal sex life with your partner is your birthright. Step into it, right now, and enjoy!

Affirmations when properly done always work!
(although not always within our preferred time frame or the way we think they should work)

SKIN (DRY/IRRITATED)

One of the side effects of chemotherapy can be dry and irritated skin. Take extra care of your skin a week or two before you begin your chemo treatments. If your skin becomes too dry, it can be prone to infection. The following practical tips may help you to minimize skin damage and discomfort:

- Take shorter showers or baths.
- Always use a very gentle fragrance-free soap, laundry detergent and dishwashing soap.
- Moisturize your skin with creams or ointment. I found coconut oil to be the best.
- Wear wide-brimmed hats and sunglasses when outside in the sun.

It's best to stay out of the sun, if possible. If you have to be in the sun, protect your skin. When my skin became itchy, I applied a cold cloth and then gently massaged in some coconut oil.

A good way to start your day...

Look in the mirror and affirm that your face is clear and healthy. Thank it for serving you well for all these years. Know that it is the chemo/radiation and/or other medical treatments that is/are causing this condition of your skin being dry and irritated, and that this too shall pass! Bless your face, neck and skin and thank them for working so well for you.

Borrow Back exercise

Think of a time in your life when your skin was clear, healthy and firm. Access that memory and mentally transport it into your present moment. Remember how great you felt and the comments you received about the condition of your lovely skin and how young and healthy you looked. When you bring this vivid memory into the present, visualize it as being real. Since your subconscious mind does not know the difference between a real and an imagined event, your mind will begin to create healthier skin.

Photograph exercise

Find a photograph of yourself looking youthful, fresh-faced and healthy. Place it on a sheet of blue paper (blue represents healing). Now, imagine your face and skin being immersed in a soft golden mist of healing, with great health and vitality permeating your face, neck, shoulders, arms, legs and entire body. Feel how happy you are that your skin is becoming refreshed, invigorated and rejuvenated, right now. Visualize this healing power saturating every pore of your skin and every part of your body and imagine your skin becoming increasingly healthy and revitalized. Finish with: "Thank you, thank you, thank you," and enjoy your day, knowing that your mind is already working on your behalf.

Use your own voice recording

Listen to the audio recording that you created with your own voice and wake up trusting that your skin is already becoming healthier, firmer and younger.

Message from your affirmation life coach

Look at you! You have made wonderful progress. Don't forget to take the time to acknowledge all your efforts and gains on this challenging journey. You are taking charge of your mind—and it's working!

Affirmations when properly done always work!
(although not always within our preferred time frame or the way we think they should work)

SWALLOWING (DIFFICULTY)

Bless your pills, fluids and food

When taking your chemo pill or any other pills, food or fluids, hold them in your hands and say with great feeling: "I love you, I bless you, and I thank you for sliding down my throat easily and for going to the right places in my body for healing, for my highest good." Then focus on feeling whatever you are swallowing easily and normally going down your throat. Be aware of the relief you feel when things go down smoothly. Practise living in an attitude of gratitude, saying: "Thank you, thank you, thank you for the blessings that I have received and the ones that I am about to receive."

Borrow Back exercise

Close your eyes and mentally go back to a time when you felt radiantly healthy and happy. Your throat was clear and you were eating and swallowing normally and easily. See yourself in vivid colour and remember that feeling of ease and comfort. Allow this feeling to permeate every part of your body. To bring this image more powerfully alive, engage your senses: **see** yourself being healthy; imagine **hearing** people commenting on how great you look; **feel** gratitude; **smell** your favourite essential oil, and **taste** some fresh, sparkling water or visualize biting into a juicy apple. Now transport this beautiful, healthy image and memory into your present moment. Imagine it actually taking place right now! You are so blessed. Savour that wondrous memory and feeling for a few minutes, then open your eyes slowly and come back into the present. Know that you can always go back and access that memory whenever you wish. Keep it fresh and exciting so it will stay on the front burner of your mind.

1% Solution affirmation

Say: "Today, I am swallowing 1% more easily than I was yesterday." When your mind fully believes that statement, you can increase it and say: "Today, I am swallowing 5% (or 10%) easier than I was yesterday." Make it believable so your conscious mind will not cancel it out.

Use your own voice recording

Listen to the audio recording that you created with your own voice and wake up trusting that eating and taking your medication is going to be easy and stress-free from now on.

Message from your affirmation life coach

Feel and embrace the wonderful healing that you have affirmed and are receiving. Your throat is becoming healthy and clear, and you are swallowing easily and normally. Awesome job! I am very impressed with your commitment to using these powerful Affirmation Life Tools.

Affirmations when properly done always work!
(although not always within our preferred time frame or the way we think they should work)

WORRY AND ANXIETY

Hourglass exercise

If you don't already have an hourglass, purchase one and put it on the table or on your desk, where you can easily see it. If you become overwhelmed with worry or anxiety, turn the hourglass upside down and sit and watch as the grains of sand slowly pass through the narrow neck of the hourglass. If you tried to push too many grains of sand through at the same time, they would clog up and none would get through—or the glass would break. I liken this to my life. When I feel very anxious, I just think about that hourglass and I do one thing at a time, concentrating and focusing on it until it's done. Then I go on to the next one. If I attempt to do several tasks at the same time, I often get overwhelmed and nothing gets done. This is a very simple yet powerful exercise that will help you to pace yourself in a healthy way and avoid over-extending or stressing yourself.

Worry Drawer exercise

Make a list of everything you are worried or stressed about, being very specific. Date and sign it and then place it in a drawer. After a few months, take it out and look at it. You will realize that 90% of what you worried about never happened and the 10% that did happen was not at all affected by your worry. Worrying is a waste of precious energy that could be put to much better use, such as doing your affirmations and focusing on positive solutions.

Make a conscious decision to worry less. Worry is interest paid on trouble before it becomes due. It's like a boil coming to a painful head, often erupting into fear or panic. But worry only becomes fear if you allow it to or do not control it. Fear short-circuits the cosmic healing energy that flows throughout your body. It inhibits your cells and creates poison that can be injurious to your organs, tissues and every cell of your body. Any negative thought, if fertilized, can develop into a real fear monster that can weaken or even incapacitate you. Conquer fear by putting it into proper perspective. Worrying about things that we cannot control dissipates energy faster than we can accumulate it. Choose, instead, to channel that powerful energy into restoring your health.

Cup-emptying exercise

Take some masking tape and write on it: 'My excessive worry'. Place the tape on a cup and fill the cup with water. Sit down with it in your hands and visualize all that excessive and needless worry dripping into the cup from your eyes, ears, nose and mouth. Stay with it until you feel that you have released as much as you can, then take the cup to the sink and dump the water down the drain, knowing that you can never get that water back and that all your worries have gone with it. For optimum results, this exercise should be performed for 21 consecutive days.

Note: I read somewhere that worry is like a rocking chair; it gives you something to do but gets you nowhere! Are you overly attached to a particular outcome? If so, release that rigid attachment, right here and right now. Practise being patient, trusting that renewed health is already on its way to you.

Two of my readers—Lily and Rebecca—shared with me their experience of dealing with worry in their lives:

> *I used to worry because I had nothing to worry about. I would speculate on the negative odds of what could happen and it was beginning to make me physically ill. Now, I use the Worry Drawer exercise. I put into words what I'm worrying about, place it safely in a drawer and leave it for a period for time. Then, when I take it out and read it, it shows me with wonderful clarity what my percentages are. Yours gratefully, Lily—the Former Worry Wart.*

> *I used to worry all the time, even when things were going great. Then I took your suggestion and I wrote down everything that I was worried about, dated and signed it, and put it in a drawer. I took it out about a year later and, you know, you're absolutely right: about 90% of what I worried about did not happen and the 10% that did was not the least bit affected by my worry. So why worry?*

Some helpful tips

Anxiety can be experienced as an uneasiness, nervousness, worry or fear. It can create disturbing physical sensations, as a result of overwhelming stress or uncertainty, and can manifest in different ways for everyone. Find a technique that works for you to lower your anxiety. It might be having acupuncture treatments, meditation, doing yoga, listening to soothing music, exercising in nature, or going for a relaxing massage.

Make a habit of breathing deeply for several minutes, as often as you can, as this calms the nervous system. If your anxiety feels unmanageable, ask your doctor for a referral to a counsellor. Getting professional help for severe anxiety is as important as taking your medication.

This Too Shall Pass affirmation

This became my own personal mantra, repeated numerous times during the day. Whenever a side effect or some anxiety kicked in, I immediately affirmed: "This too shall pass." And it always did. This is a very helpful affirmation and I rely on it as one of my most effective resources. When I'm in an uncomfortable or negative situation, I simply visualize those four words, which are engraved on the back of my ring, and I instantly feel comforted by them.

Journaling

Document your healing journey. Keeping a diary or journal of how you are feeling once treatment has started is very important and helpful. The act of writing calms the mind, enabling you to focus more objectively on what is happening, while also enabling you to flag your fears as well as your progress. Things are likely to become clearer as you write, generating ideas, inspiration or solutions to your health challenges. Documenting your experience also provides you with tangible information that can be shared with your health professional, while reminding you of the steady improvements taking place.

Use your own voice recording

Listen to the audio recording that you created with your own voice and wake up trusting that your worries are being handled and you can relax.

Message from your affirmation life coach

You are learning the secret of co-creation. Consciously choosing to feel calm and content is a powerful step to take. Embrace the fact that you can release worry and anxiety so that you can focus on healing and living your life.

Affirmations when properly done always work!
(although not always within our preferred time frame or the way we think they should work)

PART THREE

5

Affirmations for other challenging situations relating to caregiving, family, career and finances

In this chapter, I've provided some affirmations and exercises for dealing with other difficult situations that may result from your diagnosis. Other key aspects of your life, such as your career, family and finances, may be severely affected by your health challenges, creating even more stress or worry for you, as well as stress and worry for your loved ones. Dealing with their concerns may add to your burden, even as they're doing their best to help you.

Many of these tools can also be used by your caregivers, your spouse or other family members to help them cope better and to help them help you in a positive, loving way, without depleting or over-extending themselves.

CAREGIVING

Sometimes, the caregiver gets overlooked in all the chaos. He/she also needs some tender, loving care and consideration to keep on going and to stay strong and healthy enough to help you. Often, both the person who is ill and their loved ones can experience fear, blame and anger when there's a diagnosis of cancer, but these emotions should not be allowed to remain after the initial shock has passed. Doctors and healthcare practitioners don't always have everything perfectly figured out, so we all need to be proactive in researching and taking responsibility for addressing the various health challenges that we or our loved ones may be facing.

Borrow Back exercise

Being a caregiver can be hard work and draining, at times. To help you cope, mentally go back to a time in your life when you felt strong, healthy and full of life. Where were you? What you were doing? Who was with you? How were you dressed? Visualize as many of the details as you can. Then transport that vivid and colourful image into the present time. Allow that feeling of strength, complete health and happiness to saturate every cell of your body, and remember how well you handled difficult situations, at that time, and how confident you felt about any task or job that you took on.

Tips for self-care

- Be good to yourself and be careful not to over-extend yourself in caring for others.
- Get enough rest and sleep as soundly as you can.
- Eat properly.
- Don't be too hard on yourself and don't feel guilty if you don't spend every minute with your loved one/patient.
- Schedule some alone time for yourself.
- Enlist the help of doctors, nurses, healthcare professionals, counsellors, family members and others who may be able to offer guidance or assistance.

Kathy Worthy, who participates in one of my chemo classes, shared with me what she does to help her cope with taking care of her husband, who is undergoing chemotherapy. She makes a point of leaving the house every day to do something special for herself, and she urges other caregivers to plan outings that are fun and doable—such as going to the local theatre, getting together with friends or organizing potluck dinners, so you don't have to do all the work. As Kathy points out, however, some people (even caring, well-meaning friends) can drain your energy with their questions and suggestions, so going to see a movie with them can be a nice way to shift the focus away from your situation and onto something more uplifting.

By taking care of her own needs in a healthy way, Kathy is learning to receive, not just give, as she knows the importance of receiving in maintaining a healthy flow and exchange of energy.

If this is the first time you find yourself in a caregiving situation, be patient with yourself and the person you're helping. Remind yourself that there's no point in making yourself ill by over-extending yourself for someone else.

Use your own voice recording

Listen to the audio recording that you created with your own voice and wake up trusting that you will stay strong, positive and mindful of having healthy boundaries around caring for others.

Message from your affirmation life coach

You are using your skills to the good of all, and I applaud you! You are caring for your loved one/patient with love, patience and tenderness, while still taking good care of yourself. I am so proud of you!

Affirmations when properly done always work!
(although not always within our preferred time frame or the way we think they should work)

FAMILY DIFFICULTIES

When a family member has been diagnosed with cancer or any other serious medical condition, it may be time to do a Master Family Affirmation to help you all cope. It may also be beneficial to call a family meeting (depending on the age of the children), to explain and discuss the best possible way to deal with what is taking place. When things are explained openly, honestly and simply, this helps the family to pull together as a unit. This could help make family members a little kinder, considerate and more loving. If Mom or Dad gets sick, it is hard on everyone. Work with your own family dynamics, but be open and up-front with your children and any other family members who may be worried or stressed.

The following affirmation provides a sample of the kind of wording you can use to make your own.

Master affirmation for families

We know our family is facing an uncertain situation and/or health challenge, right now. We decide as a family to work together to get through this family crisis as easily and quickly as possible. First and foremost, we remember to always be kind, loving and considerate with one another and to help out with household chores etc, as much as possible. We strive to be positive and upbeat. As a family, we pray and affirm together for the highest and best outcome for everyone and we are grateful.

Family meeting

It can be a good idea to call a family meeting, as having an open, honest discussion about what's going on usually helps to allay everyone's fears or panic. Have a short agenda prepared so you know what points you wish to cover. Depending on the family members and the age of your children, you may wish to share with them all or some of the information about the cancer diagnosis that you or your loved one has been given. It is usually a good idea to share some of the proposed treatments and some of the expected side effects, so that everyone is prepared—and better able to help if they're not taken by surprise. I would suggest that you not go into great detail, at the first family meeting; just give enough information so your family members are aware of the cancer diagnosis and/or chemo treatment and have an idea of what to expect. Be open to answering questions and explain your answers as clearly as you can. Then end the meeting on a positive note and talk about plans for family trips and gatherings when the treatment is finished and the patient has recovered.

Note: Each family member has to deal with his or her own feelings, while trying to be sensitive to the person with cancer or other health challenge. Some members of the family are able to absorb the impact of the cancer diagnosis more quickly than others. Maintain normal living and daily routines as much as possible during this challenging time, as this usually helps everyone involved to feel more secure.

Picture Power exercise

Find a nice colour photo of your family, with everyone smiling and happy. Stick the photo on your fridge, where everyone can see it, and write below it: 'Our family is now loving, harmonious and working together through this health challenge.' As you look at the picture, feel the warmth and loving kindness of your family members.

Cancel, Cancel affirmation

If a family member says something negative to you, just say to yourself: "Cancel, cancel. That's not true!" Then immediately replace that thought with a positive statement, such as: "I am happy, well and secure." It's important to immediately fill that space with something positive as nature abhors a vacuum and your mind may rush to fill it with something you don't necessarily want.

Use your own voice recording

Listen to the audio recording that you created with your own voice and wake up trusting that things are working out perfectly, and that you and your family are taken care of.

Message from your affirmation life coach

You are a wonderful leader and it is time to trust your own decisions. Your family is now starting to work together as a team to get through this medical challenge.

Affirmations when properly done always work!
(although not always within our preferred time frame or the way we think they should work)

CAREER

Having cancer or some other serious health issue can play havoc with your or your partner's career and/or your ability to earn a living. If you are undergoing chemotherapy, radiation or other medical treatments, you may need to take time off for treatments and, subsequently, for recovery, while also dealing with ongoing pain, discomfort and nausea. Use some of the following Affirmation Life Tools to help you cope and to restore your health and vitality as quickly as possible.

Mentally Accept the Worst exercise

Take a few moments to mentally accept the worst-case scenario, given your current situation, then immediately start to improve upon it. Focus your mind on finding ways to mitigate, stop or handle the challenges that you face, so you don't panic. Think of ways you could work with your employer to keep your position and keep on receiving the money you need for yourself and/or your family. If that is not an option, remember that you are trained and capable in many ways. There is always some solution out there, if you are determined to find a way to make things work. Trust yourself and explore all opportunities, keeping an open mind and a positive spirit. Then allow yourself to move forward whichever way you feel led.

Use the following affirmation to keep you focused on your ideal situation, with regard to your work or career.

Master affirmation for career

I, [your name], *deserve and now have—and continue to have— the perfect, lasting, successful career/job for me. I receive in excess of $_____ monthly/yearly (net or gross). My employer is sympathetic to my current health challenge and works with me to help me cope successfully. I use my creative abilities and enjoy harmonious working conditions with everyone involved. We are fulfilled, to the good of all parties concerned. I fully accept. Thank you, thank you, thank you.*

Note: When you date and sign this Master Affirmation, you have made a firm and binding contract with God, your higher self or whomever/whatever you believe in. Make it as enthusiastic, detailed and colourful as you can, to keep the mind engaged, energized and working on your behalf. (Colour wakes up and excites the subconscious mind and helps your affirmation to manifest quicker.)

Act As If exercise

When you have created your Master Affirmation and created a practice of reading it twice daily, it's time to 'act as if' you already have the perfect, lasting, successful career that you desire. Your mind will take note of your actions, which demonstrate your clear intention to accept and receive what you're affirming, and it will go about creating the conditions required to bring it to fruition.

Use your own voice recording

Listen to the audio recording that you created with your own voice and wake up knowing that you are creating that wonderful, successful and lasting career.

Message from your affirmation life coach

You have affirmed and ordered up your perfect, lasting, successful career and it is time to accept and enjoy it. I am so impressed with your courage and determination.

Affirmations when properly done always work!
(although not always within our preferred time frame or the way we think they should work)

FINANCES

When a family member is diagnosed with cancer or some other serious medical condition, he or she may have to take time off work to undergo chemotherapy or other treatments. Consequently, the family may be faced with a loss of income. I recommend using the money Affirmation Life Tools to help generate extra money during this difficult time.

Magic Magnetic Health Circle affirmation

Stand in front of the window and, with your arms outstretched from your sides, turn slowly clockwise while saying these words: "I, [your name], now magnetize into my Magic Magnetic Health Circle [aura] from the sun, moon, stars and entire solar system great abundance in all parts of my life. Money flows to me in streams of abundant wealth. Thank you, thank you, thank you." Do this procedure slowly three times, allowing each word to sink deep into your subconscious mind, where all creation begins.

Master affirmation for money

I, [your name], deserve to be and am becoming wealthier and wealthier. Money is my friend. I respect it and it respects me. I write 'thank you' three times on my cheques, bills and invoices when paying them. I know that financial abundance relieves stress. It gives me the freedom to pay all my bills and obligations and have money left over for vacations and whatever I wish to purchase. Money gives me financial security and enables me to help others. My family and I are safe, protected and financially blessed. Money is constantly circulating in my life. I use it wisely and constructively to help family, self and others. We are all happy, healthy and prosperous, to the good of all parties concerned. Thank you, thank you, thank you.

Other simple things you can do to attract more money

- **Make yourself a magnet for money.** Whenever you're exercising, walking or waiting in line somewhere, keep repeating to yourself: "I am a powerful money magnet!"
- **Doodle dollar signs ($)** any time you're sitting at your desk or waiting for a client or friend to arrive. This gives your subconscious mind an image upon which to focus and keeps your intention on the front

burner of your mind. Get excited! Think about what you will do with that money, and make a list so that it becomes more real in your mind.

- **Plant your own money tree.** Purchase a small tree and plant it in your backyard where you can visualize taking money from it. If you don't have the space outside, plant a small tree in a pot in your home or make one from material. Place dollar bills on it, using clothespins or paper clips to attach the bills to the branches or leaves. If you are unable to do it with real money, take pieces of paper and put the amounts you wish to see multiplied: $50, $100, $5,000, $l00,000 or more. You can also use monopoly or play money. Visualize yourself picking all the money you desire—$10s, $20s, $50s, $100s, $1000s—from your very own money tree.

There is always a money tree in my home, and it has a powerfully positive influence in my life. If you create your own money tree, you will find that you start attracting opportunities, support and positions that you never dreamed possible.

Use your own voice recording

Listen to the audio recording that you created with your own voice and wake up trusting that you now have a powerful new consciousness of financial abundance, which is already working in your favour.

Message from your affirmation life coach

You are a powerful money magnet, attracting opportunities, people and situations that bring money to you, in all kinds of positive and unexpected ways. If you keep this up, I know you will continue to reap the wonderful benefits.

Affirmations when properly done always work!
(although not always within our preferred time frame or the way we think they should work)

Dealing with the diagnosis of cancer and how I successfully used these tools to restore my health

Cancer is a blow to every family it touches. It can generate a lot of fear, as well as disrupting careers, families and daily routines. A husband whose wife has been diagnosed with cancer and is undergoing treatments may find himself coming home from work, preparing dinner, helping children with homework, changing bedding and doing all the tasks that his wife would usually do but is now too ill to accomplish. If the husband of a stay-at-home wife gets cancer, the wife may find it necessary to seek employment outside the home, as well as doing all her usual household tasks.

With so many logistical challenges to be faced, in addition to addressing the cancer itself, it's important to not let fear consume you. It's also important to be as well informed as possible, since misinformation or a lack of knowledge can feed our fears. I heard of one employee, for example, who was afraid of catching cancer from a fellow worker and requested a separate bathroom.

Don't get too caught up in statistics or averages, as no two cancers have ever acted exactly the same way. Each one of us has different genes and immune systems. Focus on the many promising results that cancer patients have obtained, trust in the power of your mind to heal your body, and use your own creativity in applying the Affirmation Life Tools to address your own particular health needs.

Fear of cancer and treatment

Fear of cancer is largely a fear of the unknown, as we do not know everything about cancer or even what's happening inside our own bodies. However, much research has been done and new and effective treatments are being developed all the time. It is usually easier to cope with the known than the unknown, because we at least have an idea of what to expect. Knowledge helps release fear. Think of chemo and other medical treatments as friends who are helping you, or as your personal weapons for attacking and warding off the enemy. You are taking control of your life, not submitting.

Dealing with fear is a key focus in the Affirmation Life Tools that I've developed. During chemotherapy, I often found myself projecting into the future, imagining all sorts of negative impacts. *How will this affect my family? What about our finances? Will I have to quit my career? Will I ever be able to use my fingers properly again? Will I ever be able to walk and move easily? What if I do not feel like having sex? Will I be able to travel? How will people accept me in this compromised health situation? When will it end?*

As I mentioned earlier, I found that every side effect generated a fear of me being permanently damaged or incapacitated. Whenever that happened, I immediately used my Fear Dragon exercise to help calm me down and disperse that intense fear.

Getting rid of anxiety

In considering and undergoing chemotherapy, I had to release the memories of many former unpleasant experiences of going for doctors' appointments. I gave a command to those negative thoughts, telling them they had to go and allow new, happy and positive ones to take their place. Instead of dreading the visits to my doctor, I mentally anticipated feeling very calm and having a positive, successful visit. I believe that positive, healthy affirmations are commands that direct the body's healing forces to function at peak performance. Positive, happy imagery accelerates the body's healing process and, in some cases, results in cancer remission.

Nourishing my body

I made sure that I ate something nourishing before my chemo intravenous treatments so that my body was as fortified as possible. I stocked up on chicken soup and other items that calmed my stomach. I discovered that if I sucked an ice cube while the intravenous chemo solution was entering my veins, it reduced my mouth sores and discomfort.

It's important to be present

Life is like a smorgasbord. You can sit all day and wait for a person to serve you, but you must take the appropriate action—get up and help yourself!

I took control of my life and stopped concentrating and thinking in terms of 'what if...?' or 'I should have...'.

I stopped postponing my health or happiness until some future time. Instead of telling myself that I would be happy when my operation was over or my chemo was complete, I focused on being as happy as I could in every moment.

Some of the Affirmation Life Tools that I used during my health challenges

All these tools are designed to help you handle the unpleasant side effects of chemo or other treatments. They will not necessarily make the side effects magically disappear (although they often do), but they will help to calm you down, give you hope and something positive upon which to focus your mind. When you repeat these positive, uplifting words over and over, they sink deep into your subconscious mind where they can take root, grow and manifest the positive results that you seek. Make up your own affirmations and have fun! The more enthusiastic and lighthearted you can be (even though that can be extremely difficult when you're feeling very ill), the more likely you are to generate a positive outcome.

Swallowing a Whole Apple exercise

I used this exercise to help me cope when I had emergency surgery, was diagnosed with colon cancer, developed a severe infection, took chemo and then lost my husband in the middle of my treatments.

I realized that I simply couldn't deal with everything at once. It was like trying to swallow an apple whole. If I did that, I would choke, but if I cut the apple up into small pieces, I could complete the task of eating it. So I visualized cutting up into sections my health challenges and my husband's death. Then I took one section at a time and put it in order so I could deal with it more easily. When I did this, my mind was able to think realistically and rationally. I started to think about what I could do about each situation that would be positive and help me cope. In the process, I realized that I was overly attached to having certain outcomes, so I released my attachment to things unfolding a certain way and kept affirming that they would work out for my highest good. I coped and still am coping, thanks to the lesson of the apple! This simple process worked wonders for me and gave me a great deal of peace.

Block of Ice exercise

I started this exercise by visualizing in my mind a square block of ice. Then I mentally began chiselling out the image of self that I desired. This was quite easy for me to do as my first husband was a famous chef and regularly did wonderful ice carvings for special banquets. Each day, I worked at it a little at a time. I found that my affirmations and exercises kept me busy, so I did not have so much time to worry or fret about the future. After a few weeks, a vibrantly healthy image of me began to emerge from that block of ice!

This tool helped me cope with the side effects of chemotherapy. I used it, for example, when my hair was thinning and becoming limp and lifeless, when I had red, angry blotches on my face, when my skin was very dry and flaky, and when I was unsteady on my feet and felt weak, frail and lacking in self-confidence.

First, I focused on my thinning hair and visualized the block of ice as having my strong, healthy, shiny, thick hair hidden deep within it. Then I mentally chipped away all the excess ice and, to my amazement and delight, I uncovered an image of my strong, healthy, thick hair. I held onto that image and focused on it every time I started worrying about that condition. I soon forgot about my thinning hair as I had replaced those negative thoughts with my positive, vivid, healthy image.

Then I went on to the next nasty side effect, doing the same thing for my skin, weight, balance and self-confidence. I did the same chiselling process to uncover a colourful image of me looking healthy, happy and cancer-free. This process quickly became one of my favourite and most successful tools. It worked miracles for me, and I continue to use it whenever the need arises.

Note: The timing of my success varied. Sometimes, it worked immediately; at other times, it took a little longer—perhaps a day or a week. However, I feel that the time frame was dependent upon my faith and enthusiasm at that time, and I now endeavour to do this exercise as energetically and creatively as possible.

Creative Anti-cancer Visualization exercise

I visualized the cancer drugs that I was receiving as poisoning the cancer cells and then imagined ALL my healthy cells joining together to fight to eradicate every trace of cancer from every part of my body. One of my friends visualized her radiation treatments as huge beams of energy and light bombarding every cancer cell like a rocket. In my mind's eye, I saw my healthy blood cells as highly trained and skilled doctors who were finding and getting rid of all the cancer cells in my body. Be creative with this concept. With a little practice, you will develop the approach and creative imagery that work best for you.

Eggshell affirmation

I took a clean, empty eggshell and placed some short-form affirmations in one half of it, on little pieces of paper. Then I taped the eggshell together again and planted it in the rich, fertile soil of my flower garden. I did this knowing that the shell would disintegrate and get absorbed into the soil, along with my printed affirmations, which would take root, grow and manifest my desires. As I planted the eggshell in the soil, I said: "Thank you, thank you, thank you for manifesting my desires, as affirmed, for my highest good." Then, every time I passed by my flower garden, I made a point of saying thank you. I found this affirmation to also be a powerful faith-builder, due to the physical process of planting my words in the soil and seeing my flowers grow.

Here are some of the short-form affirmations that I placed in that eggshell:
- I am a survivor.
- I am cancer-free.
- I am well.
- I am happy.

Toothbrush Forgiveness affirmation

When you brush your teeth, look at yourself in the mirror and say: "Hey, self, you are a mighty fine person" or "You are beautiful/handsome." Then say: "I, [*your name*], now forgive everyone and everything that has *ever* hurt me. I now forgive myself and am forgiven. I love, respect, accept and approve of myself just the way I am. [Visualize and imagine your entire body becoming clear, pure and healthy.] Thank you, thank you, thank you." Use this process every time you brush your teeth.

Note: When you do this exercise, your mind may bring up some of the people, situations or events that have hurt you. If this happens, and if too many unhappy, negative thoughts come to mind at the same time, just say, with authority: "One a time, please!" Then forgive each one completely before going on to the next one.

I used this affirmation repeatedly to forgive many things—myself, for not taking better care of my health; the cancer; the negative side effects of chemo and the pain, nausea and suffering that I experienced; feeling sorry for myself and just about everything that upset me. Then I focused on loving, respecting, accepting and approving of myself and my decisions. Loving myself just as I was (am) proved quite challenging, at times, but repeating the affirmation over and over proved very helpful and uplifting for me, especially through the most difficult phase of treatment and the loss of my beloved husband. It is my hope that it will help you just as much, if not more, with your health challenges.

Affirmation Life Tools work with children, too!

Children have no skepticism. They are open to learning new things and have wonderfully vivid imaginations, coupled with their innate ability to visualize. One day, when I was teaching the Toothbrush Affirmation Life Tool to a Grade 3 class in Washington State, we were all standing outside after class and Tommy, one of the students, said, "Dr Evers, I can't do that Toothbrush thing." I said, "Why not, Tommy?" He looked down as he kicked the dirt and said in a low voice, "Because I don't love myself." My heart went out to him and I said, "Promise me that you will do it anyway, until I come back next month, and then tell me about it." He said, "Okay" and ran to catch the school bus. When I returned a month later and was walking down the hallway, Tommy spotted me, broke away from his classmates and came running up to me. "I did it! I did it!" he said. I had to think for a moment or so and then I said, "What did you do, Tommy?" He said, "What you told me to do—you know, that toothbrush thing." With his eyes sparkling and with great excitement, he proclaimed, "And I love myself!" I said, "Oh, Tommy, I am so proud of you!" He impressed and touched me even more when he added, "And I love and respect others, too."

I could share many other wonderful stories from children who have used these simple tools and transformed their thinking and actions. There are two other examples that stand out in my mind: Daniel, who was known as the class bully, stopped fighting other kids when he understood the ripple effect of his actions and the importance of respecting others; and Lindy, who visualized talking to a friendly giraffe as part of the Fear Zoo exercise, overcame her fear of heights.

Fear Dragon exercise

Imagine your fear in front of you in the form of a dragon. How big is it? What colour is it? What shape is it? How close is it? Can you feel its breath? How hot is it? Do you feel uncomfortable?

Now imagine picking up a club and pushing the fear dragon away from you. You are stronger than any of your fears. Ask the dragon to speak to you. Say: "Have you anything to say to me?" Listen with your inner ears. You may be surprised by what it says to you. Be firm with the fear dragon and inform it that it has no place in your healthy body or around you and that it has to go. Should it try to hang around, say again: "You must go now! You are not welcome in or around me. You have no power over me. I am the powerful force here and you must obey me. I am the boss." Be firm and the dragon will vanish completely. Now, in the empty space that you have just created, place a colourful image of what you wish to feel like or accomplish. This tool is very effective in banishing any limiting fears and helping you to achieve what you desire.

Robert, a businessman in England, shared his experience with doing this simple exercise.

I used this exercise in facing my fear of poverty, which I called the 'Poverty Fear Dragon'. In my mind, I looked at it square in the face and demanded that it leave now. It wanted to hang around but I told it I was in control. Since then, I found a new job with more money, better, benefits and more secuity. Thank you!

Hourglass exercise

When I think about all the work I need to complete and I glance about my office and see piles of paper and numerous e-mails that need attention, I often feel overwhelmed and paralysed. But I have a solution for that! On my desk, I have an hourglass. Whenever overwhelm kicks in, I turn the hourglass upside down and watch the tiny grains of sand filtering through the narrow glass neck. I know that if I tried to push too many grains of sand through at once, they would get stuck and none would come through. This principle reminds me that I must do the same thing with my life and work. So I pick one e-mail at a time and completely focus on the question and my answer to it. When I feel I have accessed the correct information, I check it and send it. Then I go on to the next one, with a sense of control and accomplishment, even though I've only completed one small task.

This Too Shall Pass affirmation

When I experienced a negative side effect, I immediately said: "This side effect is not coming from my body. It is coming from the chemo treatment and it is only temporary. This too shall pass." I used this particular affirmation so much that it became my constant mantra.

Affirmations when properly done always work!
(although not always within our preferred time frame or the way we think they should work)

Short-form affirmations

Agreement from your body

I now have a perfect and total health agreement with every part of my body.

Brain

I have a healthy brain/mind that operates perfectly.
All of my brain chemo fog has now lifted completely.

Ears

My ears are healthy and working perfectly.
I now hear clearly and distinctly.

Energy

I feel increased energy flowing throughout my body.
Wondrous, healing energy is now saturating every cell of my body.

Eyes

I have perfect 20/20 vision.
I see clearly now.

Hair

Every strand of my hair is healthy, thick and beautiful.
My hair grows long, strong and healthy.

Healing

I give myself permission to accept my wonderful healing!
All pain, tension and negative stress now leave my body.
I am completely healed in every part of my body.

Health (general)

It is my birthright to be healthy, wealthy and happy, and I accept it now.
I feel healing energy saturating every cell and tissue of my body.
All my cells are restored to perfect health.

Heart

My heart is disease-free and working perfectly.
My heart is strong and healthy.

Immune system and cells

My cells are now becoming healthy, normal and energized.
My immune system grows stronger every day.

Love

I love, respect, accept and approve of myself, just as I am.
Loving myself promotes healthy conditions in my body.

Meditation

My regular meditation promotes good health in my body and mind.
I meditate on health, peace, joy and happiness.

Mind

My mind and brain are filled with wondrous healing.
My memory is sharp, healthy and accurate.

Pain

All pain leaves my body now and I am pain-free.
I love being relaxed, comfortable and pain-free.

Releasing

I now forgive everyone and everything that has ever hurt me.
I forgive myself and am forgiven.

Worry

I release all worry from my body.
I am calm and worry-free.

Affirmations when properly done always work!
(although not always within our preferred time frame or the way we
think they should work)

Testimonials

I can usually tell by a patient's mental attitude if he/she will complete their chemo treatments. I was amazed at how Anne Marie's affirmation teachings transformed the lives of my patients. I was also very impressed at how Anne Marie could go through everything she did—having colon cancer, getting a serious infection, undergoing chemo and then suffering the terrible shock of the sudden death of her husband—and still give back to others by conducting monthly lectures and sharing her Affirmation Life Tools with chemo patients to help them cope with the side effects.

— **Dr Sasha Smiljanic**, chemotherapy doctor

I think positive, uplifting affirmations are very helpful to everyone, but especially those living with cancer or other health challenges, those undergoing chemotherapy, and those in the last phase of life. A positive, uplifting approach helps to make the days meaningful and peaceful, while also providing a means of coming to terms with the realities of life.

—**Dr Paul Sugar,** palliative-care doctor

[Note from Anne Marie: Anita is a very vibrant, lovely young lady who was diagnosed with breast cancer and had numerous chemotherapy and radiation sessions. She says that cancer bestowed many gifts and blessings upon her and she urges others to look ahead beyond the 'eye of the storm' when they are in the midst of cancer treatments. Cancer taught her to be a gracious receiver. She had to learn to sit back and let her family and friends love and help her.]

I have used and am using Anne Marie's 'Clear, Search and Retrieve' exercise to help me cope with chemo brain fog and it is working great. I also use her 'STOP sign' process and I find that it actually stops the pain for several hours! I am so grateful for these exercises and the many other useful tools that Anne Marie teaches. I would not know what to do without them.

—**Anita MacAulay, chemo patient at Lions Gate Hospital, Vancouver, BC**

[Note from Anne Marie: I had the privilege of meeting both Ewa and her husband Roman at my home about a year ago. I watched her as she embraced the affirmation process and saw how she blossomed. She easily adapted to using these Affirmation Life Tools. Now, she has a spring in her step and a renewed zest for life. I am so proud of her and her vast achievements. I am thankful that Iris Enkurs gave me the opportunity to meet her as Ewa and Roman are now like part of my family.]

Five years ago, I was diagnosed with breast cancer. I went through the usual triple-treatment—surgery, radiation and chemotherapy. Unfortunately, the cancer spread to my bones and life took a very different turn. I felt very depressed and not hopeful about my future. On one of my lowest days, I went to the chemo clinic and was advised by my doctor to talk to the social worker in the unit. In our conversation and in an attempt to help me, Iris, the social worker, mentioned Dr Anne Marie Evers. She thought that Anne Marie, known for her optimism and strategies for dealing with cancer, could be a good resource for me.

So then I got to know Anne Marie and read her book, Affirmations: Your Passport to Happiness, *focusing particularly on the chapters dealing with health. In the beginning, I was skeptical but I decided to give it a try. I prepared my Master Affirmation, glued a picture of me healthy and relaxed above it, and repeated the affirmation out loud in the morning and evening. After a while, I noticed that my mental clouds, which were bereft of hope, slowly began to lift and optimism took their place. I used affirmations during stressful moments, such as waiting for a CT scan. Sitting in a hospital gown, I kept repeating to myself that the cancer cells were decreasing in my body and that the scan was going to look better than the previous one. This made me feel empowered and less scared.*

Through affirmations, I have also incorporated other important factors in life such as concern about others and gratitude for everything I receive. The illness deepened my understanding of what is important in life and woke up a desire in me to live as fully as I can.

— **Ewa Izdebski**, cancer/chemo patient

I think what you are doing is wonderful! So much of what you have written resonates with what I did when I had to deal with breast cancer a few years ago.

—**Glenda Ponroy, France**

Words cannot describe how your teachings have helped me and become a huge part of my life. It was affirmations that helped me cope with my busy career as a Registered Nurse, as well as a severe head injury suffered by my husband.

I have been an RN for 34 years and can bear testimony of the power of affirmations. I have watched people survive cancer, chemo and life-threatening illnesses, but the oncology patients who had positive thoughts and attitudes

typically endured their treatments better and seemed to improve more rapidly. I believe your book will help countless people worldwide. Thank you so much for your valued help and caring, and for bringing affirmations to light in my life.
—**Carolyn Walsh, RN, Texas, USA**

Anne Marie has triumphed over personal heartbreak at many stages of her life, using the techniques she shares in this powerful book. Each painful experience has contributed to the integrity of her teachings, magnifying her ability to create joy, health, hope and happiness from human tragedy. You don't need to feel helpless or powerless while coping with illness—yours or anyone else's. This book will support, comfort and guide you through your darkest days, providing inspiration and practical tools for regaining your health. Anne Marie has been a guiding force of light in my life. I invite you to allow this light to illuminate your path so you may discover the love, laughter, joy, hope and healing within these pages.
—**Kate Large, author of *Waiting in the Other Room* and founder of The Game of Life Mastery Program**
www.TheGameofLifeMastery.com

I have written out many affirmations and have received almost everything I asked for. The most important affirmation I did was asking for healing for myself when I was diagnosed with colon cancer. It was a very frightening experience. Fortunately for me, I was able to phone my dear friend Anne Marie and ask for help. She told me to write out the following words seven times every morning and evening, for the seven days before my operation: "My operation is a success. I am radiantly healthy."

I then had to have radiation treatments for six weeks, and it was very scary being in a room by myself with this huge machine descending down on me. To keep from being afraid, I visualized myself playing golf at my favourite golf course. It worked! I got my mind focusing on and thinking about something positive and happy. I still write this affirmation every day, seven times: "I am abundantly healthy and happy." Thank you, thank you, thank you, Anne Marie for helping me with your affirmations at the most important time of my life.
—**Caroline Ryker, Bellingham, WA**

I have been a social worker at Lions Gate Hospital in North Vancouver, BC, for about 25 years and feel very privileged to work in the hospital's chemotherapy clinic. Every one of our patients has lived a remarkable life yet cancer has cast a challenging shadow over their life journeys. Chemo treatments can be rough and emotions can run raw. Sometimes it can be hard to find the energy to put one foot in front of the other. I have been very impressed at Anne Marie's consistently cheerful presence, her genuine caring for others, and her passion for sharing her Affirmation Life Tools. Not only did she use them herself, but she was enthusiastic about teaching other interested patients/family members how to use them as well. It's been wonderful for me to see how receptive people have been to learning and working with these tools. She is one amazing lady, and I'm sure you will enjoy her positive uplifting energy as she guides you to learn these tools, too.

—Iris Enkurs, MSW, RSW

*When someone hears those three words—*You have cancer*—there are three possible reactions: they can ignore it, give up or prepare to wage the battle of their lives. All cures start with positive attitudes and beliefs. Cancer can be beaten and patients can regain their health. There is no such thing as false hope. I am very impressed by Dr Anne Marie Evers and her positive affirmations. They go a long way towards helping patients rally their physical, mental, emotional and spiritual resources through the power of the word. Her book is for just about anyone with any kind of chronic medical condition. I particularly liked the Flashlight Affirmation Tool. It's brilliant, simple and fun!*

—Roxanne Davies, writer/researcher, Vancouver, BC

Anything produced by Anne Marie Evers is guaranteed to lift your heart and make you feel better—and this book is no exception. Filled with inspiring stories, timeless wisdom and lovingly-worded affirmations for all situations, it's an emotional 'first-aid kit' that helps you to create magic in your relationships, finances, career and health. It's practical, positive and simple to use. Highly recommended as a powerful healing tonic for whatever health challenges you may face.

—Olga Sheean, Empowerment Coach and author of *The Alphabet of Powerful Existence*

Author's message

Thank you for joining me on this journey of discovering the hidden power within you to heal yourself using these Affirmation Life Tools. I have thoroughly enjoyed sharing my experiences with you and I hope you have found hope, inspiration and a renewed faith in yourself to create the health and life you desire.

It is my sincere hope that these Affirmation Life Tools have helped you with any health challenges you, your loved ones or your friends may be going through—and that it will serve you again, should the need arise. I urge you to keep this book handy so you can refer to it often and remind yourself of the limitless power of your subconscious mind. These tools are simple and a wondrous gift that you can take with you and use at any time, in every situation of your life.

To find out more about the power of properly done affirmations, you can read my first book, *Affirmations: Your Passport to Happiness, 8th Edition*, which is available on www.amazon.com.

Additional Affirmation Life Tools available free of charge:

- A free e-book version of this book is available on my websites: www.annemarieevers.com & www.annemariesangelchapel.com
- You may sign up for the 74-day e-course: 'Affirmation Life Tools help you cope with chemo and/or other medical treatments', and receive these tools in your inbox daily. This very popular e-course will be regularly re-run. Please check my website for updates.
- An audio book on Affirmation Life Tools for coping with chemo and other medical treatments will be released in mid-2015.
- You can receive free daily affirmations in your inbox. Please sign up on www.annemarieevers.com.

With gratitude, love and many affirmation blessings,

Anne Marie

Website: www.annemarieevers.com
E-mail: annemarieevers@shaw.ca

Affirmations when properly done always work!
(although not always within our preferred time frame or the way we think they should work)

NOTES FROM THE AUTHOR

June, 2016

Canadian Conference of Community Oncology

I was honoured and pleased to be invited to lecture on my Affirmation Life Tools Help Cope with Negative Side Effects of Chemo and/or Other Medical Treatments on June 20, 2015 at the Canadian Conference of Community Oncology at the Four Seasons Hotel in Whistler, BC Canada.

Lions Gate Hospital

l began lecturing at Lions Gate Hospital, North Vancouver, BC, Canada on the power of Affirmation Life Tools on September 26, 2014 and these lectures are ongoing on the last Friday of every month.

New Website

Please take a few moments to check out my new website: www.heretohelpsolutions.com and watch the very short, colourful and snappy videos on Affirmation Life Tools and videos on Coping with Chemo and End of Life Information — together with suggested various Affirmations.

Your Affirmation Life Coach

Anne Marie